GEORGE F. KENNAN

Recent Titles in Bibliographies of American Notables

John C. Calhoun: A Bibliography
Clyde N. Wilson

GEORGE F. KENNAN

An Annotated Bibliography

Compiled by
Laurel F. Franklin

Bibliographies of American Notables, Number 3
Mary Ellen McElligott, Series Editor

GREENWOOD PRESS
Westport, Connecticut • London

Library of Congress Cataloging-in-Publication Data

Franklin, Laurel F.
George F. Kennan—an annotated bibliography / compiled by Laurel F. Franklin.
p. cm.—(Bibliographies of American notables, ISSN 1091–8302; no. 3
Includes indexes.

1. Kennan, George Frost, 1904– —Bibliography. 2. United States—Foreign relations—Soviet Union—Bibliography. 3. Soviet Union—Foreign relations—United States—Bibliography. 4. United States—Foreign relations—1945–1989—Bibliography. 5. Cold War—Bibliography. I. Title. II. Series.
Z8462.75.K75F73 1997
016.32773047—dc21 96–51785

British Library Cataloguing in Publication Data is available.

Library of Congress Catalog Card Number: 96–51785
ISBN: 978-0-313-28306-2
ISSN: 1091–8302

First published in 1997

Greenwood Press, 88 Post Road West, Westport, CT 06881
An imprint of Greenwood Publishing Group, Inc.

Printed in the United States of America

The paper used in this book complies with the Permanent Paper Standard issued by the National Information Standards Organization (Z39.48–1984).

10 9 8 7 6 5 4 3 2 1

CONTENTS

PREFACE

My own interest in George F. Kennan began while I was a graduate student and working librarian at The City College of the City University of New York. By that time, the Vietnam War was over, but its influence was still present and palpable. The study of American foreign relations, and containment policy was a way to try to find answers to the plaguing question of how and why this event had occurred.

This bibliography would never have been begun without the inspired teaching of Professor Jim Watts of The City College History Department, who showed me the joys and rewards of research in American foreign policy. I thank the librarians in the following institutions for assistance in this project: The New York Public Research Libraries, Columbia University Libraries, the Mudd Manuscript Library at Princeton University, and the George C. Marshall Research Library. My colleagues at The City College Library have been very helpful, and I am particularly obligated to all of them in the Interlibrary Loan Division.

Finally, this work would never have been completed without the unfailing support of my husband, Woody, who also helped with translations and provided invaluable assistance with preparation of the manuscript.

INTRODUCTION

The writings of George F. Kennan--diplomat, historian and Soviet expert--are a rich source for anyone trying to understand 20th century U.S. diplomacy, and in particular the intellectual and policy struggles surrounding the Cold War. This is not to suggest that Kennan's interests fall within a narrow range: they run from academic history to critiques of current policy. The variety of his topics is rivaled by the diversity of forums in which they are presented. The works of the scholar sit side by side with those of, and for, the engaged citizen.

This remarkable output reflects Kennan's crucial, paradoxical blend of the policymaker at the heart of practical debate, and the observer keenly aware of his outsider status.

Most prolific at a time when the U.S. was consolidating its position as a dominant world power at the height of the Cold War, Kennan has remained part of debate on key foreign policy issues from that time to the present. But Kennan's depth of historical perspective, and his practical knowledge of the workings of world power, give even the most topical of his interventions enduring resonance. His early insights into nations and policies are borne out, in today's rapid change, in ways the Cold War's stasis did not permit, and lesser Cold Warriors never imagined.

U.S.-Soviet relations, diplomacy, the arms race, nuclear weapons strategy, and U.S. reliance on militarization, are major themes found here. Through these analyses, Kennan probed beyond Cold War dichotomies, recognizing no simple solution to international problems in a "victory" of one side over the other. He saw that the Cold War was in many ways a convenience for both sides in avoiding harder and more lasting issues. These enduring issues have been a constant theme in his works.

Thus, for example, to read Kennan's Reith Lectures today is to recognize that his concern over the solidification of a divided Germany and the repercussions of that unreal state of affairs were not unfounded. Kennan is almost alone, in the Cold War years, in his refusal to take for granted a divided Europe--this even as he fully recognized balance-of-power realities. His position to many at the time seemed impossibly abstract: the current wisdom was that the alternative to a divided Germany and a divided Europe would be Western vulnerability to Soviet pressure and subversion. But Kennan's approach to the problem grew out of a subtle appreciation for the underlying problems of mutual security on the Continent. The theme is pursued throughout the years, with variations in emphasis.

Many of Kennan's writings, and much of the critical analysis cited here, debate Kennan's own role in the containment policy of the late 1940s through the 1980s. With the publication of the "X" article in 1947, in which Kennan's usage of "containment" provided the label for the policy that the U.S. would follow over the next forty years, he has been identified with containment policy. The citations here reflect the centrality of containment to U.S. post-war policies; they also indicate the development of the policy to its nadir in the Vietnam War. Clearly his part in the formula has been a troublesome one for Kennan and he has struggled to clarify his original meaning ever since. But what could be a merely verbal quarrel has served to bring out nuances of policy and historical perspective that help to shed light on a contentious era.

Kennan's realist philosophy is also much debated, and his writings looked to for counsel on the proper role of the U.S. in international affairs. Again the question is timely. What are U.S. objectives, and how ought they to be carried out? Kennan's attempts to define the limitations of American power and influence are still significant. In an age where U.S. omnipotence seems less and less obvious, his guarded perspective seems increasingly at home.

For some time, Kennan has engaged in debates about nuclear weapons policy, campaigning against nuclear proliferation and for a U.S. "no first use" policy. His writings convey that the nuclear weapon is different in kind, not simply in degree, and that its proliferation has an uncontrollable life of its own. Whereas the Cold War provided reasons or excuses to evade these issues, its end has placed them, too, high on the public agenda.

Kennan is also concerned with U.S. society at large. And again, not unexpectedly, his role is that of the "outsider" to received opinion. Not only is he concerned about the deleterious effects of technology and the rapid pace of environmental change, he is impatient with the shortcomings of a democracy in conducting its foreign affairs and solving its problems. Kennan is among the few with the temerity to suggest Constitutional revision to improve this state of affairs. Whatever one may think of Kennan's self-confessed elitism and dislike of much of modern-day life, here he once again shows his readiness to take up unpopular positions.

COVERAGE

This is an annotated bibliography of published books and articles by and about George F. Kennan. It does not include unpublished works in archival collections. The coverage is, for the most part, of works in English, although a few foreign language works are included, as are translations of Kennan's major works.

The first section, of works by Kennan, is intended to be comprehensive only as to books and journal articles. A few of the most significant newspaper articles are included; or brief excerpts of such articles found in readily available publications. Reprints are cross-referenced to the original appearance of a text. Book reviews are included, but not always annotated. U.S. Documents are listed, but coverage is highly selective. These include Congressional hearings, the *Foreign Relations of the United States* (FRUS) series, and others. Short comments, such as introductions and letters to the editor, are listed in the section labeled COMMENTARIES.

The second section, of works about Kennan, includes articles, biographies, and monographs with substantial sections on Kennan. In general, reviews of Kennan's works are not included, although there are some review-essays. This section is selective, with an emphasis on recent opinion and comment. The range of works, however, provides differing interpretations and gives an overview of the historiographical developments in Cold War history.

Annotations are intended to be informative rather than critical. They are based on a reading of the work itself, or an edition of the work. Many editions and a few works have not been seen; this is indicated after the citation.

CHRONOLOGY

1904	b. Milwaukee, Wisc., Feb. 16
1921	Graduates from St. John's Military Academy, Delafield, Wisc.
1925	Graduates from Princeton Univ., B.A.
1925	(summer) Seaman on coastal vessel
1926	Accepted for Foreign Service School
1927	Vice Consul in Hamburg
1928	Vice Consul in Tallinn
1929-1931	Third Secretary in American Legation, Baltic States; Language Officer, Berlin; academic study in Seminary for Oriental Languages, Berlin
1930	Diploma from Berlin Seminary for Oriental Languages
1931	Marries Annelise Sorensen
1931-1933	Third Secretary, Riga consulate
1933-1934	Third Secretary, Moscow (under William C. Bullitt, first U.S. Ambassador to Soviet Union.)
1935-1937	Second Secretary, Moscow
1937-1938	Russian Desk, State Dept., Washington, D.C.
1938-1939	Second Secretary and Consul, Prague

1939-1941	Second Secretary and First Secretary, Berlin
Dec. 1941- May 1942	Interned at Bad Nauheim, Germany
1941-1943	Counselor of Legation, Lisbon
1944-1946	Minister-Counselor, Moscow (under Averell Harriman and Gen. Walter Bedell Smith)
1946-1947	State Dept.'s Deputy for Foreign Affairs at the National War College, lecturing on foreign affairs
1947-1949	Chief of Policy Planning Staff, State Dept.
1950	Counselor, State Dept., Washington, D. C.
1950-1951	Leave of absence from State Dept. to Institute for Advanced Study, Princeton, N.J.
1952	Ambassador to Soviet Union
July 1953	Retires from Foreign Service
1953-1955	Member of the Institute for Advanced Study
1956-1974	Permanent Professor in School of Historical Studies, Institute for Advanced Study
1957	National Book Award; Bancroft Prize; Pulitzer Prize, History, for *Russia Leaves the War* (1956)
1957-1958	George Eastman Visiting Professor, Balliol College, Oxford Univ.
1957	BBC Reith Lecturer
1961-1963	Ambassador to Yugoslavia
1965-1968	President, National Institute of Arts and Letters
1966-1970	University Fellow in History and Slavic Civilizations, Harvard Univ.
1967-1971	President, American Academy of Arts and Letters
1968	Pulitzer Prize, Biography; National Book Award, for *Memoirs 1925-1950*
1969	Fellow, All Souls College, Oxford Univ.
1974- present	Professor Emeritus, Institute for Advanced Study

1974-1975	Fellow, Woodrow Wilson International Center for Scholars, Washington, D.C.
1975	Founder, Kennan Institute for Advanced Russian Studies, Washington, D.C.
1981	Albert Einstein Peace Prize; Grenville Clark Prize
1982	Peace Prize of the West German Book Trade
1988	Toynbee Award
1989	Presidential Medal of Freedom

WORKS BY GEORGE F. KENNAN

1942

ARTICLES

1. "Report: The Internment and Repatriation of the American Official Group in Germany, 1941-1942." Parts 1 and 2. *American Foreign Service Journal* 19 (Aug./Sept. 1942): 422-426+, 473-477+.

The official report on the internment of U.S. Embassy personnel on the outbreak of war with Germany, Dec. 11, 1941. Kennan describes the journey to Bad Nauheim, organization and daily life of the internees, and removal to Portugal prior to repatriation.

1947

ARTICLES

2. "The Sources of Soviet Conduct." [X.] *Foreign Affairs* 25 (July 1947): 566-582.

The famous and influential article, published anonymously by Kennan, who was soon identified as its author. Kennan proposes "containment" of communist expansion, analyzes Soviet behavior in terms of Russian history and psychology--a search for security, secretiveness, distrust of foreign influence--and details Soviet vulnerabilities which will lead either to "mellowing" or a breakup of the Soviet system. Communist ideology is a barrier to understanding between the Soviets and the West, and a challenge to the U.S. (Hereafter referred to as the "X" article.) (Reprinted nos. **4,46,203-204,218,283,319,378,391-392,405,413,451,479,558,613, 628.**)

3. "University Education and the Foreign Service." *American Foreign Service Journal* 24 (May 1947): 7-9, 36.

Outlines qualities and education a Foreign Service Officer should have. Kennan also remarks that the newly established National War College will provide a consistent viewpoint on global problems for policy-makers in various branches of government.

REPRINTS

4. *The Sources of Soviet Conduct.* [X.] New York, 1947. 19p.
(Not seen. Reprint of the 1947 article, no. **2**.)

1948

ARTICLES

5. "The United States and the United Nations: Proceed with Patience, Confidence and Realism." *Vital Speeches of the Day*, 15 Nov. 1948, 68-70.
Making the United Nations into an effective peacekeeping organization will be difficult, but the U.S. should work toward this end, for the common good and for its own self-interest.

1949

DOCUMENTS

6. "The International Situation." *Department of State Bulletin*, 5 Sept. 1949, 323-324. (S1.3)
A brief review of postwar recovery. Kennan sees a need for a strong military as long as the free world is under political attack but does not rule out co-existence. [An address over the Columbia Broadcasting System, Aug. 22, 1949.]

REPRINTS

7. "How to Meet the Soviet Challenge." *U.S. News & World Report*, 18 Feb. 1949, 36-40.
(Abridgement of the 1947 article, "The Sources of Soviet Conduct," no. **2**.)

1950

ARTICLES

8. "Foreign Aid in the Framework of National Policy." *Proceedings of the Academy of Political Science* 23 (Jan. 1950): 448-458.
Foreign aid is neither charitable giving, nor a panacea. It is in the national interest, and as such is indispensable in improving the U.S. image abroad and assisting those peoples resisting communism.
[Speech at the Dinner session of the Annual Meeting, Nov. 10, 1949.]
(Reprinted **17**.)

9. "Germany-Soviet Union." *American Foreign Service Journal* 27 (Feb. 1950): 25+.
An analysis of Nazi foreign policy in light of captured documents. Kennan sees evidence of a German-Soviet pact that predated the Munich agreement, refuting claims of Soviet apologists who cite Munich as a cause of the pact.

10. "The Great Issues of American Life, 1925-1950." *Current Religious Thought* 10 (Oct. 1950): 3-6.

Dilemmas faced by modern man are the relationship of individual man to organized society--man's manipulation of the masses, and man's control over nature--and the looming possibility of environmental destruction. The U.S. must look to method, as well as purpose, in achieving its goals.
[Baccalaureate address, Dartmouth.]

11. "Russia and the United States." *New Republic*, 16 June 1950, 12-16.
The manichean view of communism prevalent in the U.S. is not constructive in understanding the movement, the Russian Revolution, or the Russian people. Russia after the revolution contains some traditional elements as well as new responses to modern problems. The "witch hunting" in the U.S. only reinforces the attitude that evil is something entirely outside ourselves. Deeper understanding of the weaknesses that contribute to totalitarianism is necessary.
(Reprinted no. **20**.)

DOCUMENTS

12. "Current Problems in the Conduct of Foreign Policy." *Department of State Bulletin*, 15 May 1950, 747-751+. (S1.3)
Kennan defends the State Department's stewardship of policies toward the Soviet Union and China, and deplores attacks on the integrity of individuals in the Department. In such attacks, our basic values of tolerance and free inquiry are endangered.
(Reprinted nos. **16,19,21**.)
[Address before the Institute on U.S. Foreign Policy in Milwaukee, May 5, 1950.]

13. "Is War with Russia Inevitable?" *Department of State Bulletin*, 20 Feb. 1950, 267-271. (S1.3)
Soviet ideology does not call for war, Kennan says, and he deplores war-scare talk on both sides. But the Soviets are attempting political expansion of communism, and for this reason, the U.S. should continue the policy of containment. The only alternatives would be isolation or war. Important aspects of national security policy are a strong military, aid to our allies, attention to our own domestic problems, and a spirit of justice and goodwill.
(Reprinted nos. **18,44**.)

COMMENTARIES

14. "Leland Morris." *American Foreign Service Journal* 27 (Aug. 1950): 14.
Kennan's tribute to a colleague with whom he had served in Berlin in 1940-1941.

15. "Pakistan-United States Relations." In *Pakistan: The Heart of Asia, Speeches in the United States and Canada May and June 1950*, by Liaquat Ali Khan, 137-140. Cambridge, Mass.: Harvard Univ. Press, 1950.
In this Epilogue to a collection of speeches by the Prime Minister of Pakistan, Kennan notes the evident disparities between the strength of the U.S. and new nations such as Pakistan. He calls for new foreign policies, and recognition of its responsibilities on the part of the U.S.
[Address before the Foreign Policy Association, New York, May 8, 1950.]

REPRINTS

16. *Current Problems in the Conduct of Foreign Policy.* Washington, D.C.: U.S. Dept. of State, Office of Public Affairs, 1950. 15p. (U.S. Dept. of State Publication 3862. General Foreign Policy Series, 31.) (S1.71:no. 31.)
(Reprint of the 1950 document, no. **12**.)

17. "Guide to Giving." *Time*, 23 Jan. 1950, 10.
(Excerpt from the 1950 article "Foreign Aid in the Framework of National Policy," no. **8**.)

18. "Is War with Russia Inevitable? Five Solid Arguments for Peace." *Reader's Digest*, Mar. 1950, 1-9.
This article, originally written for *Reader's Digest*, was first published in the *Department of State Bulletin* in Feb. 1950.
(Reprint of the 1950 article, no. **13**.)

19. "Kennan Stresses Depth of Forces Shaping World Events." *Foreign Policy Bulletin*, 19 May 1950, 1-3.
(Abridgement of the 1950 article "Current Problems in the Conduct of Foreign Policy," no. **12**.)

20. *Russia and the United States, a Speech Delivered at the Annual Student-Faculty Banquet, Russian Institute Student Group, Columbia University, May 27, 1950.* Stamford, Conn.: Overbrook Press, 1950. 18p.
(Not seen. Reprint of the 1950 article, no. **11**.)

21. "The Situation in the Far East." In *Problems of Asia: An NBC Radio Discussion*, 14-17. Chicago: Univ. of Chicago, 1950. (University of Chicago Roundtable, no. 648, Aug. 27, 1950.)
(Excerpt from the 1950 article "Current Problems in the Conduct of Foreign Policy," no. **12**.)

1951

BOOKS

22. *American Diplomacy, 1900-1950.* Chicago: Univ. of Chicago Press, 1951. ix, 154p. (Charles R. Walgreen Foundation Lectures.)
Six lectures in which Kennan talks about "legalism" and "moralism" as the underlying concept in U.S. foreign policy, and approaches questions of the national interest and policy-making in a democracy. The lectures illustrating his themes are on the Spanish-American War, the Open Door policy, policy in the Orient, World War I, World War II, and modern diplomacy. Contains reprints of the "X" article, (no. **2**) and "America and the Russian Future," (no. **25**).
(Reprinted nos. **42-43,60-61,82,157,216,236,252,274,354,363**. Excerpts reprinted nos. **86,131,240,258,388a**. See also no. **525**.)

23. ______. Collector's ed. Chicago: Univ. of Chicago Press, 1951. ix, 154p. (Charles R. Walgreen Foundation Lectures.)
(Not seen.)

24. ______. New York: New American Library, 1951. 127p. (Charles R. Walgreen Foundation Lectures.)
(Not seen.)

ARTICLES

25. "America and the Russian Future." *Foreign Affairs* 29 (Apr. 1951): 351-370.
A Russia freed from communism will not develop into a mirror-image of the U.S. The totalitarian state is inherently weak, but change, to be lasting, should come from within the U.S.S.R. The U.S. should beware of specific commitments to liberation, and be aware of the potential for national and ethnic clashes. The most powerful influence the U.S. can have for change in Russia by its own example.
(Reprinted in *American Diplomacy, 1900-1950*, no. **22** and other eds., and reprinted nos. **30,41,579**.)

26. "Lectures on Foreign Policy." *Illinois Law Review* 45 (Jan./Feb. 1951): 718-742.
Two addresses given at Northwestern University. In the first, Kennan identifies three problems which are different from those of the past: population growth, technological weapons of destruction and control, and the challenge to the liberal philosophy of government posed by an increasingly complex society. The second address relates the national interest to national purpose rather than altruism. Kennan suggests a foreign policy based on a realistic modesty about the U.S. role in international affairs. He rebuts the charge of "isolationism" and deplores the self-righteous attacks on government officials.
(Reprinted nos. **31,33,45**.)

27. "Let Peace Not Die of Neglect." *New York Times Magazine*, 25 Feb. 1951, 10,38+.
Noting the confusion surrounding U.S. policies toward the Soviet Union, Kennan details some reasons why peace may be hard to achieve--hostility of the U.S.S.R., their military and atomic power, the inability of the U.N. to find solutions to all problems--but says these things are neither unexpected nor are they reasons to succumb to a war mentality. It is the critics of co-existence who are not realistic, in failing to look for "long-term requirements of a relationship with Communist power short of major war."
[Roosevelt Day Dinner speech, New York City.]
(Reprinted nos. **32,389**.)

28. "Where Do You Stand on Communism?" *New York Times Magazine*, 27 May 1951, 7,48+.
Written in reply to a question he received when nominated to the Princeton Board of Trustees, Kennan's stance is that reaction to Americans who are communists or sympathizers should be restrained rather than repressive, and should set an example of committment to democracy.
(Reprinted no. **62**.)

TRANSLATIONS

29. *U.S.A. und die Zukunft der U.S.S.R.* Vienna, ECA Mission für Österreich, 1951. 62p.
(Not seen. Tr. of the 1951 article "America and the Russian Future," no. **25**.)

REPRINTS

30. *America and the Russian Future*. [New York: Council on Foreign Relations, 1951.] pp. 352-370.

(Not seen. Offprint of the 1951 article, no. **25**.)

31. "How New Are Our Problems?" *Foreign Service Journal* 28 (Oct. 1951): 20-21+.

(Abrigement of the first part of the 1951 article "Lectures on Foreign Policy," no. **26**. See also no. **33**.)

32. "Let Peace Not Die of Neglect." *Reader's Digest*, July 1951, 137-138.

(Reprint of the 1951 article, no. **27**.)

33. "The National Interest of the United States." *Foreign Service Journal* 28 (Nov. 1951): 16-17+.

(Abridgement of the second part of the 1951 article "Lectures on Foreign Policy," no. **26**. See also no. **31**.)

1952

COMMENTARIES

34. "Responsibility in Government." Letter to the editor. *Time*, 29 Dec. 1952, 4-5.

Defends John P. Davies from *Time*'s accusation he misrepresented Gen. MacArthur's position on withdrawal of U.S. forces from Korea.

35. "Statement by Ambassador George F. Kennan." *Department of State Bulletin*, 21 Apr. 1952, 643.

In this brief press release on taking the oath of office as Ambassador to the U.S.S.R., Kennan expresses his desire to help to reduce tensions as he implements U.S. policies.

TRANSLATIONS

36. *Amerika Gaiko Goju-Nen*. Translated by Shin'ichi Kondo with Toji Iida. Tokyo: Iwanami Shoten, 1952. 187p.

(Not seen. Tr. of the 1951 work *American Diplomacy, 1900-1950*, no. **22**.)

37. *Amerikas Aussenpolitik, 1900 bis 1950, und ihre Stellung zur Sowjet-Macht*. With a foreword to the German edition by Felix Somary. Translated by Ernst Doblhofer. Zürich: Europa, 1952. 167, 11p.

(Not seen. Tr. of the 1951 work *American Diplomacy 1900-1950*, no. **22**.)

38. *Amerikas Aussenpolitik, 1900 bis 1950, und ihre Stellung zur Sowjet-Macht*. Translated by Ernst Doblhofer. Stuttgart: Europa, 1952. 168p.

(Not seen. Tr. of the 1951 work *American Diplomacy 1900-1950*, no. **22**.)

39. *La Diplomatie Américaine 1900-1950*. Translated by Hélène Claireau. Preface by Raymond Aron. Paris: Calmann-Lévy, 1952. 209p.

(Not seen. Tr. of the 1951 work *American Diplomacy 1900-1950*, no. **22**.)

40. *Diplomazia Americana 1900-1950.* Translated by Bruno Tasso. Milan: Garzanti, 1952. viii, 177p.

(Not seen. Tr. of the 1951 work *American Diplomacy 1900-1950*, no. **22.**)

REPRINTS

41. "America and the Russian Future." *Panorama: Revista Interamericana de Cultura* 1 (1952): 9-27.

(Reprint of the 1951 article, no. **25.**)

42. *American Diplomacy, 1900-1950.* New York: New American Library, 1952. 127p. (Charles R. Walgreen Foundation Lectures.)

(Another ed. of the 1951 work, no. **22.**)

43. ______. London: Secker & Warburg, 1952. 146p. (Charles R. Walgreen Foundation Lectures.)

(Not seen. Another ed. of the 1951 work, no. **22.**)

44. "Is War with Russia Inevitable? Five Solid Arguments for Peace." In *Readings in International Relations*, edited by Frederick H. Hartmann, 259-267. New York: McGraw-Hill, 1952.

(Reprint of the 1950 article, no. **13.**)

45. "The National Interest of the United States." In *The Age of Danger: Major Speeches on American Problems*, edited by Harold F. Harding, 80-85. New York: Random House, 1952.

(Abridgement of the last part of the 1951 article "Lectures on Foreign Policy," no. **26.**)

46. "The Sources of Soviet Conduct." In *Readings in International Relations*, edited by Frederick H. Hartmann, 238-245. New York: McGraw-Hill, 1952.

(Abridgement of the 1947 article, no. **2.**)

1953

ARTICLES

47. "Can We Avoid War with Russia?" *New Republic*, 2 Feb. 1953, 13-17.

The hostility and ideological opposition of the Soviets makes dealing with them difficult. But neither ignoring them nor belligerence is the answer. The U.S. needs to cultivate its own strength, set an example, and at the same time be ready to negotiate on specific issues. The recent malicious attacks on the loyalty of the civil service are detrimental to U.S. strength and unity.

[Speech given before the Pennsylvania State Bar Association.]

(An abridged version of the 1953 reprint "Soviet-American Relations," no. **67.**)

48. "The Climate of Current Investigations of Communism: Effect on the Colleges and the Liberal Arts." *Vital Speeches of the Day*, 15 June 1953, 539-541.

A forceful speech against current anti-communist agitation and investigations, which Kennan sees as stifling intellectual and cultural activity, the spirit of inquiry and innovation. The anti-communist forces play on materialsm and conformity.

From a talk at the dedication of the new Liberal Arts Center at Notre Dame University, on May 15.
[Address at Notre Dame.]
(See, for a different version the 1953 article "Seek the Finer Flavor," no. **52**. Reprinted nos. **63,65-66,68, 83.**)

49. "The Growth of the Soviet Threat." *Johns Hopkins Magazine* (Oct. 1953): 10-11+.
The Soviet Union began as an ideological threat to the West, at a time when the West was weak and disunited. Now that the U.S.S.R can be seen as a conventional great power, the threat is a military one. But Soviet ideology holds no attraction for Europe, and the Soviets face internal crises. Communism still has an appeal in Asia, spurred by a rejection of Western colonialism. Nevertheless, the best weapon the West has against communism is its own unity and example.
[Address at Johns Hopkins.]
(Abridgement of a talk at Johns Hopkins, published in 1954 as: "The Soviet Union and the Non-Communist World in Historical Perspective," no. **85**. See also "The Nature of the Challenge," no. **50** and "Russia and the West," no. **51**).

50. "The Nature of the Challenge." *New Republic*, 24 Aug. 1953, 9-12.
[Address at Johns Hopkins.]
(Abridgement of "The Soviet Union and the Non-Communist World in Historical Perspective," no. **85**. See also "The Growth of the Soviet Threat," no. **49**, and "Russia and the West," no. **51**.)

51. "Russia and the West." *New Leader*, 24 Aug. 1953, 2-6.
[Address at Johns Hopkins.]
(Abridgement of "The Soviet Union and the Non-Communist World in Historical Perspective," no. **85**. See also "The Growth of the Soviet Threat," no. **49** and "The Nature of the Challenge," no. **50**.)

52. "Seek the Finer Flavor." *Saturday Review*, 30 May 1953, 20, 38.
[Address at Notre Dame.]
(See, for a different version "Climate of Current Investigations of Communism," no. **48**. Reprinted no. **84**.)

53. "Training for Statesmanship." *Atlantic*, May 1953, 40-43.
Good character and good grounding in the humanities are essential for aspiring diplomats. International affairs is not a science but does require understanding man as a "political animal." Americans are averse to recognizing power, but such an understanding would be useful in counteracting tendencies toward utopianism. Kennan also touches on loyalty investigations in the State Dept., seeing them as more harmful than any alleged communist influence.
[Address to Princeton Alumni.]
(Reprinted nos. **64,96,162**.)

BOOK REVIEWS

54. Review of *The Incompatible Allies: A Memoir History of German-Soviet Relations, 1918-1941*, by Gustav Hilger and Alfred G. Meyer. *New York Herald Tribune Book Review*, 1 Nov. 1953, 4.

55. "Did Stalin's Death Change Anything?" Review of *Russia: What Next?* by Isaac Deutscher. *The Reporter*, 7 July 1953, 32-35.

COMMENTARIES

56. "Career of John P. Davies." Letter to the editor. *New York Times*, 17 Dec. 1953, 36.

Kennan defends the loyalty and integrity of Davies, a member of Kennan's Policy Planning Staff in the State Dept.

57. "No Concessions, No Concessions, No Concessions." *American Library Association Bulletin* 47 (Nov. 1953): 470.

Kennan endorses intellectual freedom, specifically deploring censorship of communist publications in libraries.

TRANSLATIONS

58. *Amerikansk Utrikespolitik 1900-1950.* Translated by Jane Lundblad. Stockholm: Tiden, 1953. 185p.

(Not seen. Tr. of the 1951 work *American Diplomacy, 1900-1950*, no. **22.**)

59. *Wu Shih Nien Lai Ti Mei Kuo Wei Chiao.* Translated by Hsu Yuen-so. Taipei: China Culture Pub. Foundation, 1953. 158p.

(Not seen. Tr. of the 1951 work *American Diplomacy, 1900-1950*, no. **22.**)

REPRINTS

60. *American Diplomacy, 1900-1950.* Chicago: Univ. of Chicago Press, 1953. ix, 146p. (Charles R. Walgreen Foundation Lectures.)

(Not seen. Another ed. of the 1951 work, no. **22.**)

61. ______. New York: New American Library, 1953, c1951. 144p. (Charles R. Walgreen Foundation Lectures.)

(Another ed. of the 1951 work, no. **22.**)

62. "The American Position on Communism?" In *Man and Modern Society: Conflict and Choice in the Industrial Era*, edited by Karl De Schweinitz and Kenneth W. Thompson, with the collaboration of Paul K. Hatt, 836-841. New York: Holt, 1953.

(Abridgement of the 1951 article "Where Do You Stand on Communism?" no. **28.**)

63. "Communism and Conformity." *Bulletin of the Atomic Scientists* 9 (Oct. 1953): 296-298+.

[Address at Notre Dame.]

(Abridgement of the 1953 article "Climate of Current Investigations of Communism," no. **48**. See also "Seek the Finer Flavor," no. **52.**)

64. "Education for Statesmanship." *Foreign Service Journal* 30 (June 1953): 18-20.

[Address to Princeton Alumni.]

(Reprint of the 1953 article "Training for Statesmanship," no. **53.**)

65. "Hope in an Age of Anxiety." *New Republic*, 1 June 1953, 14-16.
[Address at Notre Dame.]
(Abridgement of the 1953 article "Climate of Current Investigations of Communism," no. **48**. See also "Seek the Finer Flavor," no. **52**.)

66. *The Liberal Arts in Contemporary American Society*. Stamford, Conn.: Overbrook Press, 1953. 11p.
[Address at Notre Dame.]
(Not seen. Abridgement of the 1953 article "Climate of Current Investigations of Communism," no. **48**. Reprinted no. **83**. See also "Seek the Finer Flavor," no. **52**.)

67. "Soviet-American Relations: General Principles on Which to Base Policy." *Vital Speeches of the Day*, 15 Feb. 1953, 268-72.
[Address before the Pennsylvania State Bar Assn., Scranton, Jan. 16, 1953.]
(Full text version of "Can We Avoid War With Russia?" no. **47**.)

68. "The Triple Threat from Within." *New Leader*, 1 June 1953, 16-19.
[Address at Notre Dame.]
(Abridgement of the 1953 article "Climate of Current Investigations of Communism," no. **48**. See also "Seek the Finer Flavor," no. **52**.)

1954

BOOKS

69. *Das Amerikanisch-Russische Verhältnis*. Stuttgart: Deutsche Verlags-Anstalt, 1954. 96p.
[Lectures at the University of Frankfurt, summer, 1954.]
(Not seen. See also no. **73**)

70. *Realities of American Foreign Policy*. Princeton: Princeton Univ. Press, 1954. 119p. (Stafford Little Lectures at Princeton University, 1954.)
Four lectures in which Kennan discusses U.S. foreign policy. He sees a change in the concept of national interest from revolutionary times to the present, and calls for a return to policy grounded in realistic self-interest, rather than moralistic notions for making the world a better place. It is utopian to think that contractual agreements will replace "power politics." The best weapons the U.S. can use in its rivalry with the Soviets are greater self-confidence and improvements in its own society.
(Reprinted no. **300**. Portions reprinted nos. **285,303,590**.)

71. ______. London: Oxford Univ. Press, 1954. 119p. (Stafford Little Lectures at Princeton University, 1954.)
(Not seen.)

ARTICLES

72. "Amerika und Russland von Brest Litowsk bis Potsdam." *Osteuropa* 4 (Oct. 1954): 331-342.
(Not seen.)

73. "Das amerikanisch-russische Verhältnis." *Aussenpolitik* 5 (Oct. 1954): 631-642.
The fourth of four lectures given at Frankfurt University. Kennan explores the course of U.S.-Russian relations during the 20th Century and points out ways in which the American outlook was singularly unequipped to fathom Russian thinking or evaluate Russian intentions. He points out that Democrats and Republicans tended to have different blind spots, but that Americans in general shared an idealism in world affairs and a distaste for "Realpolitik," leading to disillusion and a demonization of the Soviets after the Second World War.
(See also no. **69**)

74. "Credo of a Civil Servant." *Princeton Alumni Weekly*, 2 Feb. 1954, 10-13.
Kennan's thoughts on the relevance of Christ's teachings in personal life; he talks of self-knowledge, fulfillment, and tolerance.
[Address at the Student Christian Association, Princeton University.]

75. "For the Defense of Europe: A New Approach." *New York Times Magazine*, 12 Sept. 1954, 7, 68-74.
Upon the failure of the European Defense Community, Kennan proposes an alternative security arrangement based neither on EDC nor on NATO, which will not prejudice unification of Germany.

76. "The Illusion of Security." *Atlantic*, Aug. 1954, 31-34.
Kennan links anti-communist hysteria to the country's insecurity in its new role as a world leader. The world--and the human condition--is precarious, but the answer is to maintain a sensible and healthy outlook, and to realize that total security is a fallacy.
[Commencement address at Radcliffe College.]
(Reprinted no. **260**.)

77. "Öffentliche Meinung und Aussenpolitik." *Demokratie und Aussenpolitik* 4 (1954): 8-20.
(Not seen. See also nos. **78,91**.)

78. "Öffentliche Meinung und auswärtige Politik." *Europa-Archiv* 9 (20 Feb. 1954): 6353-6360.
(See for annotation the English version published 1955 as "Public Opinion and Foreign Policy," no. **91**. See also no. **77**.)

79. "To Be or Not to Be a Christian." *Christianity and Crisis*, 3 May 1954, 51-53.
Abandoning personal moral responsibility to society, as is done in the totalitarian state, may seem an easy way out of obligations but robs individual lives of meaning.
[Sermon given at the First Presbyterian Church, Princeton.]

80. "Totalitarianism in the Modern World." In *Totalitarianism; Proceedings of a Conference Held at the American Academy of Arts and Sciences, March, 1953*, edited by Carl J. Friedrich, 17-31. Cambridge, Mass.: Harvard Univ. Press, 1954.
Sets forth characteristics of totalitarian societies and preconditions for their development. Kennan also takes up the meaning of freedom stressing that it depends upon the acceptance of restraints as well as allowing diversity. Includes transcript of discussion.

(Reprinted nos. **95,259**.)

COMMENTARIES

81. "Passage of Resolutions." Letter to the editor. *New York Times*, 25 Sept. 1954, 14. Kennan apologizes for an erroneous footnote in *Realities of American Foreign Policy* (no. **70**) which conflated two quotations from the *New York Times*.

REPRINTS

82. *American Diplomacy, 1900-1950*. New York: New American Library, 1954. 144p. (Another ed. of the 1951 work, no. **22**.)

83. "The Liberal Arts in Contemporary American Society." In *Representative American Speeches: 1953/1954*, 171-179. New York: H. W. Wilson Co., 1954.
(Reprint of the 1953 reprint no. **66**.)

84. "Seek the Finer Flavor." In *Is the Common Man Too Common?*, by Joseph Wood Krutch, et. al., 123-130. Norman: Univ. of Oklahoma Press, 1954.
(Reprint of the 1953 article, no. **52**)

85. "The Soviet Union and the Non-Communist World in Historical Perspective." In *The Threat of Soviet Imperialism*, edited by C. Grove Haines, 3-19. Baltimore: Johns Hopkins Univ. Press, 1954.
[Address at Johns Hopkins.]
(The full text of articles published in 1953: "The Growth of the Soviet Threat," no. **49**, "The Nature of the Challenge," no. **50**, and "Russia and the West," no. **51**. See no. **51** for annotation.)

86. "World War II." In *The Making of American History*, 2d. ed., rev. and enl., vol. 2, edited by Donald Sheehan, 898-912. New York: Henry Holt & Co., 1954.
Discusses prewar diplomacy, war aims and reasons for disillusionment after the war.
(Reprint of the chapter with the same title in the 1951 work, *American Diplomacy, 1900-1950*, no. **22**. Reprinted no. **240**.)

1955

ARTICLES

87. "The Challenge of Freedom." *New Leader*, 26 Dec. 1955, 11-12.
Freedom entails obligations and restraints, as well as respect for custom and tradition. It does not mean uniformity; society should recognize disparities in abilities and talents and protect variety.
[Address to Congress for Cultural Freedom, Milan.]

88. "Commencement, 1955." *Social Research* 22 (Summer 1955): 127-137.
Commercialism and materialism, pervasive in American society, are not sources of real happiness and prosperity. Americans need to take care to nurture self-fulfillment, creativity and community.
[Commencement address, New School For Social Research, June 7, 1955.]

(Reprinted no. **92.**)

89. "Comments on Ideology and Reality in the Soviet System." *Proceedings of the American Philosophical Society* 99 (Jan. 1955): 29-30.

Kennan comments on three papers on ideology and reality in the Soviet system. He notes the disparity between the utopian ideal and the reality of Soviet society, nevertheless observing that change is not impossible and negotiation is feasible. This is not the case with the Asian Communists, however.

90. "The Future of Our Professional Diplomacy." *Foreign Affairs* 33 (July 1955): 566-586.

Comments on recommendations for changes in the Foreign Service made by a committee led by Henry M. Wriston. Kennan describes the qualities he thinks a FSO should have and is critical of the committee's failure to note the harm done by security investigations.

91. "Public Opinion and Foreign Policy." In *Institutes and Their Publics: Proceedings of the International Conference of Institutes of International Affairs, New York, 1953*, 45-62. New York: Carnegie Enowment for International Peace, 1955.

Identifies factors in public opinion-making. Government plays a minor role in education on foreign policy issues, while there is great potential for commercial influence in the media. Political pressures on legislators limit Congress's ability for clear-sighted foreign policy positions and discussion.

(See also German version "Öffentliche Meinung und auswärtige Politik," no. **78.** See also no. **77.**)

92. "Speak Truth to Power." *The Progressive*, Oct. 1955, 16-18.

Containment was never meant to be primarily a military policy, contrary to implications in a recent Friends Service Committee study. Kennan takes issue with other assumptions in the study--that there is no conflict between the U.S. and the U.S.S.R., that the U.S. has a moral responsibility to provide aid to developing nations, and that violence is always unacceptable.

COMMENTARIES

93. "Dealing With Soviet Russia." Letter to the editor. *New York Times*, 6 Mar. 1955, sec. 4, 10.

Questions two recent actions of the U.S.: expulsion of the Metropolitan Boris of the Russian Orthodox Church, and barring deliveries of *Pravda* and *Izvestia*. Kennan deplores the apparent censorship exercised in these actions.

REPRINTS

94. "How Stands Our Pursuit of Happiness?" *New Leader*, 20 June 1955, 16-18.
[Commencement address, New School for Social Research, June 7, 1955.]
(Abridgement of the 1955 article,"Commencement, 1955," no. **88.**)

95. "Reflections on Totalitarianism." *Problems of Communism* 4 (Jan./Feb. 1955): 38-40.

(Reprint of the 1954 article "Totalitarianism in the Modern World." no. **80.**)

96. "Training for Statesmanship." In *Readings for Thought and Expression*, compiled by Stewart S. Morgan, John A. Hays and Fred E. Ekfelt, 42-51. New York: Macmillan, 1955.

(Reprint of the 1953 article, no. **53**.)

1956

BOOKS

97. *Soviet-American Relations, 1917-1920.* Vol.1, *Russia Leaves the War*. Princeton: Princeton Univ. Press, 1956. xiii, 544p.

A detailed history of relations between the two countries from the Bolshevik victory in Nov. 1917 to the Brest-Litovsk treaty with Germany and Russia's withdrawal from the Allied cause. Kennan rejects interpretations blaming the U.S. for strained relations at this time, but does criticize U.S. actions as "dilatory" and "ill-informed." (Reprinted nos. **323,532,574**.)

98. ______. New York: Atheneum, 1956. 544.p.

99. ______. London: Faber & Faber, 1956. xiii, 544p.
(Not seen.)

ARTICLES

100. "Americans and Russians." *New Republic*, 11 June 1956, 6.
[From a speech at the Pittsburgh Foreign Policy Association.]
(An excerpt from the 1956 article "What Should We Do About Russia?", no. **107**, see for annotation. See also no. **101**.)

101. "The Future of Soviet Communism." *New Leader*, 18 June 1956, 3-6.
[From a speech at the Pittsburgh Foreign Policy Association.]
(An excerpt from the 1956 article "What Should We Do About Russia?", no. **107**, see for annotation. See also no. **100**.)

102. "History and Diplomacy as Viewed by a Diplomatist." *Review of Politics* 18 (Apr. 1956): 170-177.

Kennan describes the task of the diplomat as a humble one, keeping crises under control and the government informed. The nature of the sovereign state--with its air of infallibility, dual motivations of national interest and party politics, alternating selfishness and idealism--means that the successful diplomat must blend idealism and skepticism.
[Paper presented at the American Historical Association meeting, Washington, D.C., Dec. 1955.]
(Reprinted nos. **118,184**.)

103. "International Exchange in the Arts." *Perspectives U.S.A.*, autumn 1956, 6-14.
Cultural exchanges are important to the U.S. for its own enrichment, not just to further policy. The U.S. could be more selective about what it exports, and more gracious in its treatment of foreign artists.
[Address sponsored by the International Council of the Museum of Modern Art,

May 12, 1955.]
(Reprinted no. **117**.)

104. "Overdue Changes in Our Foreign Policy." *Harper's*, Aug. 1956, 27-33.
Changes in Soviet leadership after Stalin's death call for revised policies, but the U.S., all along, misinterpreted Stalin's objectives and centered on winning a future war. Its own policies, the emphasis on military aid, winning over neutrals, protectionism, make it vulnerable to Soviet slogans. The U.S. needs to focus on positive policies, instead of reacting to perceived Soviet threats.
(Reprinted no. **256**. Translated no. **114**.)

105. "The Sisson Documents." *Journal of Modern History* 28 (June 1956): 130-154.
Kennan disputes the authenticity of the "Sisson Documents," which in 1918 purported to show that the Bolshevik leaders were paid agents of the German General Staff.
(Reprinted no. **301**.)

106. "The Soviet Will Never Recover," interview by Joseph Alsop. *Saturday Evening Post*, 24 Nov. 1956, 32-33+.
Kennan discusses dissent in Eastern Europe, and internal politics in the Soviet Union. Recent events in Poland and Hungary signal that Moscow is losing control in the satellite states. In Russia itself, great strides in industrialization and education make it harder for the regime to function on patterns inherited from Lenin and Stalin. Disintegration of the communist system is bound to come.

107. "What Should We Do about Russia?" *U.S. News & World Report*, 29 June 1956, 68-77.
The U.S. has concentrated its policy too much on deterring an attack by the U.S.S.R.--which was unlikely, even when Stalin was alive. Kennan suggests changes in attitude--toward normality but not intimacy in our relations with the Soviets, and more dignity and sense of purpose in our foreign aid programs. He touches on specifics, seeing no gain in opening relations with China, but advising pursuing relations with Soviet satellites, reunification of Germany, and removal of bases in Japan.
[Speech at the World Affairs Forum, Pittsburgh Foreign Policy Association.]
(Original title of speech, "Can We Do Better Than Co-Exist?" no. **116**. See also nos. **100-101**.)

DOCUMENTS

108. "Statement of Hon. George F. Kennan." In U.S. Congress. House. Committee on Foreign Affairs. *Foreign Policy and Mutual Security*. Draft report submitted to the Committee on Foreign Affairs, Dec. 24, 1956, 166-182. Washington, D.C.: GPO, 1956. (Y4.F76/1:F76/20)
Kennan talks about changes in internal operations and foreign relations of the U.S.S.R. since Stalin's death, the disintegration of monolithic communism and independent actions of satellite countries.

109. [Omitted]

COMMENTARIES

110. "Breach in the Grand Alliance." Letter to the editor. *Washington Post*, 3 Nov. 1956, sec. A, 3.

Recent U.S. actions in the United Nations, in which it allied itself in the Suez crisis with Nasser and the communist countries against Britain, France, and Israel, signals a departure from carefully constructed policy of the postwar years, an "empty legalism," and failure of communication with former allies.

111. "To Ban H-Bomb Tests." Letter to the editor. *New York Times*, 28 Oct. 1956, sec. 4, 10.

The Eisenhower Administration gives no adequate reason for rejecting Stevenson's proposal to ban testing on the hydrogen bomb, exhibiting insensivity and unconcern with a very real problem.

TRANSLATIONS

112. [Omitted]

113. *Problemy Vneshnei Politiki SSHA*. Translated by Eugene Neledinsky. New York: Chekhov Pub. House of the East European Fund, 1956. 154p.

(Not seen. Tr. of the 1954 work *Realities of American Foreign Policy*, no. **70**.)

114. "Sind Stalins Nachfölger besser?" *Die Welt*, 20 Oct. 1956, 10-11.

(Not seen. Tr. of the 1956 article "Overdue Changes in Our Foreign Policy," no. **104**.)

115. "Weiter als zur Koexistenz." *Aussenpolitik* 7 (Aug. 1956): 481-494.

(Not seen. Tr. of the 1956 article "What Should We Do About Russia?" no. **107**.)

REPRINTS

116. *Can We Do Better Than Co-Exist?* [Pittsburgh: Pittsburgh Foreign Policy Association] 1956. 21p.

[Speech at Pittsburgh Foreign Policy Association.]

(Not seen. Reprint of the 1956 article "What Should We Do About Russia?" no. **107**.)

117. *International Exchange in the Arts*. New York: The International Council of the Museum of Modern Art, 1956. 9p. [Address sponsored by the International Council of the Museum of Modern Art, May 12, 1955.]

(Reprint of the 1956 article, no. **103**.)

118. "Tidying up the Mess." *Saturday Review*, 17 Apr. 1956, 20+.

(Abridgement of the 1956 article "History and Diplomacy as Viewed By a Diplomatist," no. **102**.)

1957

ARTICLES

119. "The Awards: A Talk with George Kennan," interview by Maurice Dolbier. *New*

York Herald Tribune Book Review, 17 Mar. 1957, 2.
After receiving a National Book Award for *Russia Leaves the War* (no. **97**), Kennan talks about Wilson's diplomacy vis-à-vis the Bolsheviks.

120. "The Czechoslovak Legion." Pt. 1. *Russian Review* 16 (Oct. 1957): 3-16.
The story of the Czechoslovak Corps in Russia, 1917-1918, and of Allied policies concerning this force.
(Excerpt from *Soviet-American Relations, 1917-1920.* Vol. 2, *The Decision to Intervene*, no. **138**. See no. **141** for pt. 2.)

121. "Russia, the Atom, and the West: The Internal Soviet Scene." (The Reith Lectures - I.) *The Listener* 58 (14 Nov. 1957): 769-773.
The Soviets have achieved significant economic advances, but the internal situation is still unstable, as Khrushchev tries to assert Communist Party primacy over managers and the military.
(Reprinted in the 1958 work no. **136**. Reprinted no. **135**.)

122. "Russia, the Atom, and the West: The Soviet Mind and World Realities." (The Reith Lectures - II.) *The Listener* 58 (21 Nov., 1957): 819-822.
The threat from the Soviet Union is primarily a political one, which looks to weaknesses of Western civilization. The military threat is secondary. There is a lack of understanding between the U.S. and the Soviet Union which will not be solved by summitry and global solutions. Kennan advises concentrating on "the individual political problems."
(Reprinted in the 1958 work no. **136**. Reprinted nos. **132,135**.)

123. "Russia, the Atom, and the West: The Problem of Eastern and Central Europe." (The Reith lectures - III.) *The Listener* 58 (28 Nov. 1957): 867-870.
The situation in Eastern Europe is dangerous and unsatisfactory for all parties. Kennan urges the rethinking of western policies perpetuating a divided Germany, and suggests the possibility of mutual withdrawal of forces.
(Reprinted in the 1958 work no. **136**. Reprinted nos. **159,201,282**.)

124. "Russia, the Atom, and the West: The Military Problem." (The Reith Lectures - IV.) *The Listener* 58 (5 Dec. 1957): 907-910.
Kennan deplores the proliferation of nuclear weapons. Basing NATO defenses on tactical nuclear devices will be dangerous and will further solidify the division in Europe. He again advises mutual withdrawal of U.S. and Soviet forces from the heart of Europe, and suggests formation of paramilitary forces for defense there.
(Reprinted in the 1958 work no. **136**. Reprinted nos. **133,159,199,280**.)

125. "Russia, the Atom, and the West: The Non-European World." (The Reith Lectures - V.) *The Listener* 58 (12 Dec. 1957): 967-970.
Kennan addresses the question of foreign aid--its value and the obligation of the U.S. to provide it--and is negative on both points.
(Reprinted in the 1958 work no. **136**. Reprinted nos. **160-161,377**.)

126. "Russia, the Atom, and the West: Strengthening NATO, to What End?" (The Reith Lectures - VI.) *The Listener* 58 (19 Dec. 1957): 1015-1018.
A plea to the allies to strengthen their position through positive actions, negotiation, and greater unity, instead of relying too much on military might. Kennan recalls

his own part in role in the creation of NATO; at that time he did not view the military alliance as the cornerstone of U.S. policy it has become.
(Reprinted in the 1958 work no. **136**. Reprinted no. **160**.)

127. "When the Russians Rose Against the Czar." *New York Times Magazine*, 10 Mar. 1957, 9+.
Drawing some lessons for the U.S. policy of "liberation" from an analysis of the first (March) Russian revolution of 1917, Kennan's conclusion is that a formal victory and freedom alone were not sufficient to insure a successful democratic revolution. Cultural and political traditions are unlike those in the U.S., and are not likely to result in a U.S.-style democracy. When the time for revolution comes again, this first revolution can be an example and inspiration for a Russian-style democracy.
(Reprinted no. **202**.)

DOCUMENTS

128. "Statement of George F. Kennan." In U.S. Congress. Senate. Committee on Foreign Relations. *Control and Reduction of Armaments*. Hearings. 85th Cong., 1st sess. Pt. 11, Jan. 9-10, 1957, 997-1025. Washington, D. C.: GPO, 1957. (Y4F76/2:Ar5/4/pt.11)
Kennan says disarmament is contingent on disengagement in Central Europe; he proposes parameters for German unification, and reasons why this would serve U.S. interests. He discusses possibilities for a gradual transition in Eastern Europe and withdrawal of Soviet forces. In the Mid-East, he argues, our concern should be with the Arab governments, rather than with the Soviets.

COMMENTARIES

129. "A Fresh Look at Russia." *Foreign Policy Bulletin*, 15 June 1957, 145.
The U.S. overemphasizes Soviet militarism and overlooks the fact that situations in Third World countries which we see as Soviet aggression can result from factors which have nothing to do with communism.
[From remarks at the Overseas Press Club, New York, May 7, 1957.]

130. "History of Communism." Letter to the editor. *New York Times*, 27 Mar. 1957, 30.
Comments on an article about Theodore Draper's *The Roots of the American Communist Party*. Kennan feels the review catered only to visceral reactions to communism, ignoring the book's contribution to an intellectual understanding of the movement.

REPRINTS

131. "Conservative Empiricist." In *Documents of Modern Political Thought*, edited by Thomas E. Utley and J. Stuart Maclure, 82-86. Cambridge: Cambridge Univ. Press, 1957.
(Excerpt from the 1951 work *American Diplomacy, 1900-1950*, no. **22**.)

132. "Corruption of the Mind." *Time*, 2 Dec. 1957, 15-16.
(Excerpt from the 1957 article "Russia, the Atom, and the West: The Soviet Mind and World Realities," no. **122**.)

133. "Kennan's Plans to Avoid War." *U.S. News & World Report*, 13 Dec. 1957, 68.
(Excerpt from the 1957 article "Russia, the Atom, and the West: The Military Problem, no. **124**.)

134. *Russia, the Atom, and the West; Lectures Delivered over the Facilities of the British Broadcasting Company's Home Service, 11 November-16 December, 1957.* Princeton, N.J.: Princeton Univ. Press, 1957. 1 v. (various pagings) (The Reith Lectures, 1957.)
Brings together the Reith Lectures.
(Not seen. Reprint of the 1957 articles, nos. **121-126**.)

135. "What Khrushchev Faces Now: Slow Crisis in the Kremlin." *U.S. News & World Report*, 29 Nov. 1957, 84-85.
(Excerpts from the 1957 articles "Russia, the Atom and the West: The Internal Soviet Scene, no. **121** and "Russia, the Atom, and the West: The Soviet Mind and World Realities," no. **122**.)

1958

BOOKS

136. *Russia, the Atom, and the West.* 1st ed. New York: Harper, 1958. 116p.
A monograph collecting the 1957 Reith Lectures with the same title.
(Not seen. See nos. **121-126**. Reprinted no. **415**. Portions reprinted nos. **199,201, 377**.)

137. ______. London: Oxford University Press, 1958. 120p. (The Reith Lectures,1957.)
(Not seen.)

138. *Soviet-American Relations 1917-1920.* Vol. 2, *The Decision to Intervene*. Princeton: Princeton Univ. Press, 1958. xii, 513p.
Documents the pressures influencing Wilson's decision to send American troops to intervene in the Russian civil war in 1918, and details historical background of the internal Russian situation. Wilson took this action very reluctantly, and purposes were not very clear.
(Not seen. See no. **97** for v.1. Reprinted nos. **324, 533,575**. Excerpt reprinted no. **293**.)

139. ______. London: Faber & Faber, 1958. xii, 513p.
(Not seen.)

ARTICLES

140. "America's Administrative Response to Its World Problems." In *The American Style, Essays in Value and Performance*, edited by Elting E. Morison, 124-144. New York: Harper Bros., 1958. (American Project Series, Center for International Studies, Massachusetts Institute of Technology.)
The State Dept. organization is cumbersome, its system of analysis by consensus is stultifying and inflexible, and it is burdened by civil service requirements. Ideally, a hierarchical organization in which the Secretary of State has power over foreign affairs would be an improvement, but it is an unrealistic expectation. The Department will become of less use, and Presidents will continue to "improvise" to

get the assistance the Department should have provided.
[A report on the Dedham Conference, May 23-27, 1957.]
(Reprinted nos. **158,197,237**.)

141. "The Czechoslovak Legion." Pt. 2. *Russian Review* 17 (Jan. 1958): 11-28.
(See no. **120** for annotation.)

142. "Press Conference With George F. Kennan," interview by Kenneth W. Michael and Harry McLaughlin. *Sunday Patriot-News TV Magazine* (Harrisburg, Penn.), 7 Sept. 1958, 8-11.
Kennan explains the rationale for disengagement, and regrets the placing of atomic weapons in Western Europe and Acheson's unbending policy toward the Soviets. He answers questions about American diplomacy, and discusses China, the Mid-East and Latin America.

143. "A Reply." In *The West, the Atom, and Russia: A Round-Table Discussion of the Views of George F. Kennan*, edited by Melvin J. Lasky, 51-56. Paris: Congress for Cultural Freedom, 1958.
Kennan disputes specific points of interpretation made by discussants of his Reith Lectures, 1957, and goes on to say that recent events (the introduction of tactical nuclear weapons in NATO defenses in Europe) moot some of the premises in the lectures. He foresees a "single-minded preoccupation" with military destruction on the part of the U.S. and the U.S.S.R. if the atomic weapons race continues.

144. "The Trouble Between Britain and America." *John Bull*, 18 Jan. 1958.
(Not seen)

BOOK REVIEWS

145. Review of *Germany and the Revolution in Russia, 1915-1918*, by Z. A. B. Zeman. *Oxford Magazine*, 20 Nov. 1958, 118-119.

COMMENTARIES

146. "Below the Summit." Letter to the editor. *Time*, 23 June 1958, 2+.
Kennan objects to being included among those *Time* chastises for advocating a summit meeting on any terms.

147. "George F. Kennan Assays Quemoy," *New York Herald Tribune*, 21 Sept. 1958, 1+.
Suggests that a commitment to defend Quemoy militarily is unsound, as is the broader policy of "identification of American interests" with those of Chiang Kai-shek.

148. "Introduction." In *Siberia and the Exile System*, abridged, by George Kennan, ix-xix. Chicago: Univ. of Chicago Press, 1958.
Kennan provides historical background on the publication of this work by his grandfather's cousin, and discusses his political views, personality and literary style.

149. "The Kennan Ideas That Are Stirring Up Europe." *U.S. News & World Report*, 10 Jan. 1958, 69-70+.
An interview-style article that answers questions "in Mr. Kennan's own words from

his lectures and the . . . broadcast by the BBC" about his views on German unification, U.S. and Soviet withdrawal of troops from Europe, and nuclear capabilities.

TRANSLATIONS

150. *Roshia, Genshi, Seiho*. Translated by Saiji Hasegawa. Tokyo: Jiji Tsushin-sha, 1958. 179p.
(Not seen. Tr. of the 1958 work *Russia, the Atom, and the West*, no. **136**.)

151. *Rusland, Atomet og Vesten.* Translated by Cai Clausen. Copenhagen: Det Danske Forlag, 1958. 88p.
(Not seen. Tr. of the 1958 work *Russia, the Atom, and the West*, no. **136**.)

152. *A Rússia, o Atomo, e o Ocidente*. Translated by António Neves Pedro. Lisbõn: Ulisseia, 1958. 166p.
(Not seen. Tr. of the 1958 work *Russia, the Atom, and the West*, no. **136**.)

153. *La Russia, L'Atomo, e L'Occidente*. Translated by Francesca Ferratini. Turin: Einaudi, 1958. 110p.
(Not seen. Tr. of the 1958 work *Russia, the Atom, and the West*, no. **136**.)

154. *Russland, der Westen und die Atomwaffe*. Frankfurt: Ullstein Taschenbücher-Verlag, 1958. 126p.
(Not seen. Tr. of the 1958 work *Russia, the Atom, and the West*, no. **136**.)

155. *Ryssland, Atomvapnen, och Västmakterna*. Translated by James Rössel. Stockholm: Tiden, 1958. 135p.
(Not seen. Tr. of the 1958 work *Russia, the Atom, and the West*, no. **136**.)

156. *Sobieto Kakumei to Amerika*. Vol. 1. Translated by Mitsuhiko Murakami. Tokyo: Misuzu Shobo, 1958. 444p.
(Not seen. Tr. of the 1956 work *Soviet-American Relations, 1917-1920.* Vol. 1, *Russia Leaves the War*, no. **97**.)

REPRINTS

157. *American Diplomacy, 1900-1950*. New York: New American Library, 1958. 144p. (Charles R. Walgreen Foundation Lectures.)
(Another ed. of the 1951 work, no. **22**.)

158. "America's Administrative Response to Its World Problems." *Daedalus* 87 (spring 1958): 5-24.
(Abridgement of the 1958 article, no. **140**.)

159. "A Chance to Withdraw Our Troops in Europe." *Harper's*, Feb. 1958, 34-41.
(Excerpt from the 1957 articles "Russia, the Atom, and the West: The Problem of Eastern and Central Europe," no. **123**, and "Russia, the Atom and the West: The Military Problem," no. **124**. Reprinted no. **403**.)

160. "How Can the West Recover?" *Harper's*, Mar. 1958, 39-47.
(Excerpt from the 1957 articles "Russia, the Atom and the West: The Non-

European World," no. **125**, and "Russia, the Atom, and the West: Strengthening NATO, To What End?" no. **126**.)

161. "Should U.S. Continue Foreign Aid?" *Foreign Policy Bulletin*, 15 Apr. 1958, 117-118.
(Excerpt from the 1957 article "Russia, the Atom and the West: The Non-European World," no. **125**.)

162. "Training for Statesmanship." In *Atlantic Essays*, 3-11. Boston: Heath, 1958.
(Reprint of the 1953 article, no. **53**.)

1959

ARTICLES

163. "American Troops in Russia: The True Record." *Atlantic*, Jan. 1959, 36-42.
Kennan argues that the primary reason for American intervention in 1918-1920 in the civil war in Russia was to rescue Czech troops, who had appealed for help. He discounts a desire to overthrow the Bolsheviks as a reason for the intervention.
(Reprinted no. **355**.)

164. "Arms Control and Soviet Aims." *New Leader*, 23 Feb. 1959, 5-6.
Arms control by international agreement is made more difficult by Soviet secretiveness and the U.S. reliance on the atomic weapon, leaving too few conventional forces to bargain with. The problem of Berlin is very serious for the Soviets. Introducing atomic weapons in NATO and organizing and training West German forces raises tensions.
(Based on testimony in *Disarmament and Foreign Policy*, no. **175**.)

165. "Berlin and the Geneva Meeting." *New Leader*, 11 May 1959, 3-6.
On the eve of a "Big Four" meeting on Germany, Kennan deplores the number of interests involved and the fact that the principals are really playing to the public. But the situation is serious and talks may provide for a "cooling-off." The motivation behind the Soviet desire for talks is the realization that there will not be unification. A stark negative response on our part will not solve any problems.

166. "Disengagement Revisited." *Foreign Affairs* 37 (Jan. 1959): 187-210.
Kennan defends the concept of disengagement, answering objections raised by critics of his Reith Lectures (see nos. **121-126**, "Russia, the Atom, and the West.") The Marshall Plan and NATO should have served to make negotiation possible, by strengthening the West. But the U.S. is ignoring this opportunity. It seems to be waiting for a complete breakdown of the Soviets. Disengagement should be attempted: it would be less risky than the solidification of a divided Europe.
(Reprinted no. **404**.)

167. "Foreign Policy and Christian Conscience." *Atlantic*, May 1959, 44-49.
The question of Christian values in foreign policy is better applied to method than substance. Issues such as the Cold War, colonialism, and foreign aid are too ambiguous to assign moral superiority to one side or the other. But in the case of the atomic weapon, Christian values clearly come into play, and the U.S. must be aware of the apocalyptic dangers it brings.

[Address at the Princeton Theological Seminary.]
(A sightly different version of the 1959 article "World Problems in Christian Perspective," no. **174**. Reprinted nos. **182,239,255,342**.)

168. "History as Literature." *Encounter*, Apr. 1959, 10-16.
Kennan compares the work of the historian and literary writer. They work on different planes of reality, one concerned with external man, one with the internal being. Both are united, however, in literary effort and "the elicitation of truth."
[Based on an address to the P.E.N. Club, New York.]
(A slightly different version of the 1959 article "It's History But Is It Literature," no. **169**.)

169. "It's History, But Is It Literature?" *New York Times Book Review*, 26 Apr. 1959, 1, 34-35.
(For annotation see no. **168**. Reprinted no. **257**.)

170. "Our Aid to Russia: A Forgotten Chapter." *New York Times Magazine*, 19 July 1959, 8-9+.
Outlines the work of the American Relief Administration in the Russian famine of 1921-1922. Kennan notes that Gorki and Lenin requested aid, and that contrary to expectations of some, the ARA did not become a front for conspirators. It was an example of straightforward relations which saved millions of lives.

171. "A Proposal for Western Survival." *New Leader*, 16 Nov. 1959, 10-15.
Kennan is highly critical of U.S. policy on Germany and Berlin. Setting aside the controversial topic of disengagement, for which he had been heavily criticized after the Reith Lectures, he recommends negotiation to eliminate nuclear weapons, a more balanced attitude toward the Soviets, and a revitalization of U.S. national purpose.
[Address to the Women's National Democratic Club.]

172. "Russia, the Atom, and the West, 1959." *The Listener* 62 (29 Oct., 1959): 711-713.
Two years after the Reith Lectures, 1957 (see nos. **121-126**) Kennan finds that options have changed. Atomic weapons are now a part of NATO defenses and there is still tension around Berlin and a divided Germany. The U.S. needs a fresh approach, one not reliant on atomic diplomacy.

173. "Walter Lippmann, *The New Republic*, and the Russian Revolution." In *Walter Lippmann and His Times*, edited by Marquis Childs and James Reston, 37-59. New York: Harcourt, Brace, 1959.
Analyzes editorial opinion in the *New Republic* toward revolutionary Russia in the years 1917-1920 (during most of which time Walter Lippmann was an editor.) Although Kennan sees a misreading of the potential strength and character of the Bolsheviks, and sees flaws in the belief that, with aid and trade, Russia might become more closely linked to Europe, he allows that following Lippmann's advised course might have avoided much enmity and misunderstanding.

174. "World Problems in a Christian Perspective." *Theology Today* 16 (July 1959): 155-172.
(A slightly different version of the 1959 article "Foreign Policy and Christian Conscience," no. **167**. Reprinted no. **227**.)

[Address at the Princeton Theological Seminary.]

DOCUMENTS

175. "Statement of George Kennan." In U.S. Congress. Senate. Committee on Foreign Relations. *Disarmament and Foreign Policy*. Hearings, 86th Cong. 1st.sess. Pt. 2. Feb. 4-5, 23-26, 1959, 202-242. Washington, D.C.: GPO, 1959. (Y4F76/2:D63/3/pt.2)

There is little chance for progress in arms control without increasing conventional forces. Tactical weapons in NATO increase tensions with the Soviets. There are great risks in present U.S. policies which keep Germany divided, and contribute to the arms race.

(See also the 1959 article "Arms Control and Soviet Aims," no. **164**.)

176. U.S. Congress. Senate. Committee on Foreign Relations. *Informal Meeting with George F. Kennan*. Hearing, 86th Cong., 1st sess., May 12, 1959. Washington: D.C.: GPO, 1959. ii, 21p. (Y4F76/2:K36)

Discusses dangers from the division of Europe and proliferation of nuclear weapons, the situation in the Mid-East, problems in the U.S., and strengths and weaknesses of the Soviets.

BOOK REVIEWS

177. Review of *Efforts of Raymond Robins Toward the Recognition of Soviet Russia and the Outlawry of War, 1917-1933*, by Sister Anne Vincent Meiburger. *Russian Review* 18 (Apr. 1959): 150-151.

COMMENTARIES

178. Letter to the editor. *New Leader*, 5 Jan. 1959, 20.

Kennan rejects the conclusion in a book review of Z. E. B. Zeman's publication of documents from the German Foreign Ministry that there was significant collaboration between the Bolsheviks and the German military.

179. Letter to the editor. *New Leader*, 18 May 1959, 28.

Kennan rejects a statement in an article by Christopher Emmet, that Kennan accepts the "finality" of the status of the Soviet satellites. Kennan notes that he looks toward the possibility of greater independence for these states.

180. "Tribute to General Marshall." Letter to the editor. *New York Times*, 22 May 1959, 8.

Kennan praises Marshall's personal qualities and his achievements as Secretary of State.

TRANSLATIONS

181. *Rusia, el Atomo, y el Occidente*. Translated by Juan de la Quintana Oriol. Madrid: Europa, 1959. 158p.

(Not seen. Tr. of the 1958 work *Russia, the Atom, and the West*, no. **136**.)

REPRINTS

182. "Foreign Policy and Christian Conscience." *Fellowship*, 1 Sept. 1959, 1-7.
(Reprint of the 1959 article, no. **167**.)

183. *Foreign Policy and Christian Conscience*. With comments by Georgina Harkness, John Courtney Murray, Eugene Carson Blake, Ernest W. Lefever, Stewart Meacham. Philadelphia: Peace Education Program, American Friends Service Committee, 1959. 29p.
(Not seen. Reprint of the 1959 article, no. **167**.)

184. "History and Diplomacy as Viewed by a Diplomatist." In *Diplomacy in a Changing World*, edited by Stephen D. Kertesz and M. A. Fitzsimons, 101-108. Notre Dame, Ind.: Univ. of Notre Dame Press, 1959.
(Reprint of the 1956 article no. **102**.)

1960

BOOKS

185. *Colloques de Rheinfelden*, by Raymond Aron, George Kennan, Robert Oppenheimer, et al. Paris: Calmann-Lévy, 1960. 328p. (Collection de l'esprit.)
(Not seen. See no. **235** for annotation. Translated nos. **214,235**.)

186. *Soviet Foreign Policy*, 1917-1941. Princeton, N.J.: Van Nostrand, 1960. 192p.
A brief outline of Soviet tactics and policies, supplemented by documents: excerpts from speeches, reports and treaties. Kennan points out that the main objective during this period, that of preserving Soviet power, was achieved, but the outside world was pictured as more hostile than it really was.
(Reprinted nos. **453,467,541**.)

ARTICLES

187. "A Conversation with George Kennan," interview by Melvin J. Lasky. *Encounter*, Mar. 1960, 46-57.
Topics range from political differences between the West and the Soviet Union to Soviet historiography, and also cover American culture, the growth of technology, and Soviet motives in Hungary in 1956.
(Reprinted nos. **464,628**.)

188. "The Experience of Writing History." *Virginia Quarterly Review* 36 (spring 1960): 205-214.
Examines historical interpretation and subjectivity in recreating and comprehending the past. Kennan sees historical writing as necessary for self-knowledge and as a reminder of the restraints and limitations of the human condition.
[Address to the American Historical Society, Chicago, Dec., 1959.]
(Reprinted no. **294**.)

189. "Peaceful Coexistence: A Western View." *Foreign Affairs* 38 (Jan. 1960): 171-90.
A reply to an article by Premier Khrushchev in the Oct. 1959 *Foreign Affairs*. Kennan takes issue with his view that obstacles to co-existence all come from the West. He cites among obstructions to dialogue the Soviets' dogmatic attacks on

"capitalism" and persistent falsehoods. The real dispute is not between capitalism and socialism but between freedom and oppression. Some revision of attitudes on both sides is needed.
(Reprinted nos. **200,205.**)

190. "Soviet Historiography and America's Role in the Intervention." *American Historical Review* 65 (Jan. 1960): 302-322.
Kennan refutes the accuracy of statements made in a work by the Soviet historian S. F. Naida on the civil war in Russia, and deplores, in general, the Soviet attitude toward rules of historical evidence and the resulting unreliability of Soviet historical works.

191. "The Value of a St. John's Education." In *Speeches of Significance, Climaxing the 75th Anniversary Commencement, June 3-5, 1960*, 3-9. Delafield, Wisc.: St. John's Military Academy, 1960.
Strong conventional military forces are important, as long as total war can be avoided, making the training for them in military academies such as St. John's valuable. Just as valuable is the self-discipline and experience of working in concert with others instilled in students.

DOCUMENTS

192. "Statement of Hon. George F. Kennan." In U.S. Congress. Senate. Committee on Government Operations. Subcommittee on National Policy Machinery. *Organizing for National Security: The Department of State, the Policy Planning Staff, and the National Security Council.* Hearings, 86th Cong., 2d sess. Pt. 6. May 26, June 17 and 27, 1960, 802-850. Washington, D.C.: GPO, 1960. (Y4G74/6:N2/Se/2/pt.6)
Kennan addresses recruitment for and organization of the State Dept., internal security issues, and the role of the National Security Council in policy-making and implementation. He favors candidates with a broad background, not just technical expertise, a stronger role for the Secretary of State, and continuation of the Policy Planning Staff.
(Reprinted no. **198.**)

COMMENTARIES

193. "A Commentary." *Washington Post*, 10 Jan. 1960, sec. E, 1.
Evaluates the authenticity of a document recently smuggled out of the Soviet Union, which is critical of the Soviet regime and describes the effects of the lack of freedom of expression.

194. "Reappraising Our Position." *New York Times*, 22 May 1960, sec. 4, 2.
Deplores "deficiencies" in recent foreign policy exemplified by the U2 incident.

TRANSLATIONS

195. *Amerika und die Sowjetmacht.* Vol. 1, *Der Sieg der Revolution.* Vol. 2, *Die Entscheidung zur Intervention.* Translated by Hans Dieter Muller and Jutta and Theodor A. Knust. Stuttgart: Steingruben, 1960. 2v.
(Not seen. Tr. of *Soviet-American Relations, 1917-1920*, vols. 1 and 2, nos. **97** and **138,** respectively.)

196. [omitted.]

REPRINTS

197. "America's Administrative Response to Its World Problems." In U.S. Congress. Senate. Committee on Government Operations. Subcommittee on National Policy Machinery. *Organizing for National Security: Selected Materials*, 107-121. Washington, D.C.: GPO, 1960.

(Reprint of the 1958 article, no. **140**.)

198. "In What Way Might Our Foreign Service Be Better Prepared and Recruited, Especially in the Light of the Need for Understanding by Career Officials of Political-Military-Scientific Factors?" *Foreign Service Journal* 37 (Sept. 1960): 21-22.

This excerpt centers on recruitment and security controls for the Foreign Service.

(Excerpt from the 1960 Document "Statement of Hon. George F.Kennan," no. **192**.)

199. "The Military Problem." In *America's Foreign Policy*, edited with an introduction and notes by Harold Karan Jacobson, 433-438. New York: Random House, 1960.

(Excerpt from the 1958 work *Russia, the Atom, and the West*, no. **136**. Reprinted no. **280**.)

200. "Peaceful Coexistence: A Western View." In *Conflict and Cooperation Among Nations*, by Ivo Duchacek, with Kenneth W. Thompson, 306-313. New York: Holt Rinehart and Winston, 1960.

(Reprint of the 1960 article, no. **189**.)

201. "The Problem of Eastern and Central Europe." In *America's Foreign Policy*, edited with an introduction and notes by Harold Karan Jacobson, 423-433. New York: Random House, 1960.

(Excerpt from the 1958 work *Russia, the Atom and the West*, no. **136**. Reprinted no. **282**.)

202. "Russia Against the Czar." In *Background and Foreground: An Anthology of Articles from the New York Times Magazine*, edited with an introduction and notes by Lester Markel, 165-174. Great Neck, N.Y.: Channel Press, 1960.

(Reprint of the 1957 article, "When the Russians Rose Against the Czar," no. **127**.)

203. "The Sources of Soviet Conduct." In *America's Foreign Policy*, edited with an introduction and notes by Harold Karan Jacobson, 294-310. New York: Random House, 1960.

(Reprint of the 1947 article, no. **2**.)

204. "Soviet Advances Can Be Contained." In *Conflict and Cooperation Among Nations*, by Ivo Duchacek, with Kenneth W. Thompson, 297-303. New York: Holt, Rinehart and Winston, 1960.

(Excerpt from the 1947 article "The Sources of Soviet Conduct," no. **2**)

205. "What Chance Is There for Peaceful Coexistence?" *Reader's Digest*, Apr. 1960, 48-53.

(Excerpt from the 1960 article "Peaceful Coexistence: A Western View," no. **189**.)

1961

BOOKS

206. *Russia and the West Under Lenin and Stalin.* Boston: Little, Brown, 1961. x, 411p.
Discusses foreign relations between Russia and the West from the Bolshevik Revolution to the end of World War II, including intervention in the revolution, Russia and the Peace Conference, attempts to normalize relations in the interwar years, the Treaty of Rapallo, and Stalin's policies toward Germany and China.
[A series of lectures at Oxford and Harvard Universities 1957-1960.]
(Reprinted no. **226**. Excerpts nos. **217,219**.)

207. ______. London: Hutchinson, 1961. viii, 411p.
(Not seen.)

208. ______. New York: New American Library, 1961. 384p.
(Not seen.)

ARTICLES

209. "The American Student and Foreign Affairs." *New England Association Review* 9 (Feb. 1961): 12-13+.
A background in history and civilization, rather than attempting a specialized knowledge of current events and politics, is the best preparation for a career in diplomacy.
[Address to the New England Association of Colleges and Secondary Schools.]

210. "That Candles May Be Brought." *Encounter*, Feb., 1961, 72-74.
The greatest dangers for our civilization today are the looming possibility of total war and the stultifying effects of mass culture, not communist ideology.
[From remarks at the Congress for Cultural Freedom, Berlin.]

211. "Diplomacy As a Profession." *Foreign Service Journal* 38 (May 1961): 23-26.
A diplomat's work is partly that of analyzing a vast array of data into some coherence, and partly interpreting his own countrymen while at the same time being isolated from them. It is a way of life which will yield rewards if one believes in its value; it is not necessarily a quick route to personal advancement.
[From an address before the American Foreign Service Association.]

212. "Planning in the Department." *Foreign Service Journal* 38 (Mar. 1961): 20-22.
Kennan says the idea behind the creation of a Policy Planning Staff was a good one: to provide for formulation of overall long-range policy, bringing together information from the various geographical and functional divisions within the State Dept.
[Part of a "symposium" on the role of the Policy Planning Staff.]

BOOK REVIEWS

213. "An Historian of Potsdam and His Readers," review of *Between War and Peace: The Potsdam Conference*, by Herbert Feis. *American Slavic and East European Review* 20 (Apr. 1961): 289-294.

TRANSLATIONS

214. *Die industrielle Gesellschaft und die drei Welten; das Seminar von Rheinfelden.* [Aus dem französischen übers. von Marc René Jung] Zürich: BVZ-Verlag, 1961. 301p.
(Not seen. Tr. of the 1960 work *Colloques de Rheinfelden*, no. **185**.)

215. *Sowjetische Aussenpolitik unter Lenin und Stalin.* Translated by Pierre Mathis and Hans D. Müller. Stuttgart: Steingruben, 1961. 376p.
(Not seen. Tr. of the 1961 work *Russia and the West Under Lenin and Stalin*, no. **206**.)

REPRINTS

216. *American Diplomacy, 1900-1950.* New York: New American Library, 1961. 127p. (Charles R. Walgreen Foundation Lectures.)
(Not seen. Reprint of the 1951 work, no. **22**.)

217. "Russia and the Versailles Conference." *American Scholar* 30 (winter 1960/1961): 13-42.
Details World War I concerns of the Allied and Associated Powers over Russia, and their attempts to influence events there. Kennan is especially critical of the attempt to keep Russia in the war after 1917.
(Excerpt from the 1961 work *Russia and the West Under Lenin and Stalin*, no. **206**.)

218. "The Sources of Soviet Conduct." In *The Western World in the Twentieth Century*, edited by Bernard Wishy, 422-429. New York: Columbia Univ. Press, 1961.
(Abridgement of the 1947 article, no. **2**)

219. "Stalin and China." *Atlantic*, May 1961, 35-42.
Stalin's policies in China in the 1920's were disastrous. When the Communists did gain control under Mao Tse-Tung, it was not primarily through Moscow's efforts. China remains an "ally, but not a satellite" of the Soviets.
(Excerpt from the 1961 work *Russia and the West under Lenin and Stalin*, no. **206**)

1962

ARTICLES

220. "Contemporary Perspectives." In *Russian Foreign Policy: Essays in Historical Perspective*, edited by Ivo J. Lederer, 595-601. New Haven: Yale Univ. Press, 1962.
The Soviet Union has been a source of disruption in international politics in its challenge to the validity of the system. But there are signs of change, and of its recognition that the greatest present dangers, those of nuclear proliferation and overpopulation, demand cooperation. The U.S. needs to be ready to respond.
[An address given at a conference at Yale University, Apr., 1961.]
(Reprinted no. **253**)

COMMENTARIES

221. "Policy On Yugoslavia." Letter to the editor. *New York Times*, 2 July 1962, 28.

Speaks to a letter by Senator Proxmire, which, Kennan feels, inaccurately portrays Yugoslav influence on other neutral nations. Punitive measures against Yugoslavia will only harm U.S. interests.

222. "U.S. Shouldn't Slam Door on Yugoslavia." *Washington Post*, 8 July 1962, sec. E, 1+.

Urges the defeat of measures before Congress which would restrain aid to Yugoslavia, and deny it most-favored-nation trading status. The primary result of such acts will be only to inhibit the flexibility of American statesmen in responding to a complex, changing situation.

TRANSLATIONS

223. *Rusia y Occidente bajo Lenin y Stalin.* Translated by León Mirlas. Buenos Aires: Editorial de Educaciones Selectas, 1962. 347p.

(Not seen. Tr. of the 1961 work *Russia and the West under Lenin and Stalin*, no. **206**.)

224. *La Russie Soviétique et l'Occident; Quarante Années d'Histoire.* Translated by C.-E. Romain. Paris: Calmann-Lévy, 1962. 362p.

(Not seen. Tr. of the 1961 work *Russia and the West under Lenin and Stalin*, no. **206**.)

225. *Rusland en het Westen Onder Lenin en Stalin.* Translated by J. K. Kliphuis. Amsterdam: Becht, 1962. 357p.

(Not seen. Tr. of the 1961 work *Russia and the West under Lenin and Stalin*, no. **206**.)

REPRINTS

226. *Russia and the West Under Lenin and Stalin.* New York: New American Library, 1962. viii, 384p.

(Another ed. of the 1961 work, no. **206**)

227. "World Problems in Christian Perspective." In *American History: Recent Interpretaions*, vol. 2, ed. by Abraham S. Eisenstadt, 460-476. New York: Thomas Y. Crowell, 1962.

(Reprint of the 1959 article, no. **174**.)

1963

ARTICLES

228. "Can We Deal with Moscow?" *Saturday Evening Post*, 5 Oct. 1963, 38-43.

Differentiates between the attitudes of Moscow and Peking on nuclear war and East-West accomodation, and suggests that the U.S., without taking sides, should find a way to promote the more benign Russian views.

229. "Meet the Press: Guest George F. Kennan." Television and radio interview Aug. 18, 1963, by Elie Abel, Marquis Childs, Chalmers Roberts, Lawrence E. Spivak, and moderator Ned Brooks. Washington, D. C.: Merkle Press, 1963. 9p. (*Meet the Press*, v.7, no. 32.)

Kennan voices approval of the limited nuclear test ban treaty, and notes the influence of the Sino-Soviet conflict in Khrushchev's signing it. Other topics discussed are the Soviet satellite countries, trade with Yugoslavia, NATO plans for a multilateral nuclear force, and Kennan's proposals for troop withdrawals from central Europe.

230. "Our Foreign Policy Is Paralyzed," interview by Robert J. Moskin. *Look,* 19 Nov. 1963, 25-27.

An interview, containing summaries interspersed with quotations, made after Kennan's resignation as Ambassador to Yugoslavia. He identifies three forces hindering U.S. foreign policy: the Congress, the bureaucracy, and the self-interest of our allies. He suggests that reforms toward a parliamentary system of government would benefit our policy-making. Kennan also deplores the extreme anti-communism of the right wing (and the acquiescence of the press) which prevented, for example, trade agreements with Yugoslavia.

COMMENTARIES

231. "Ambassador Kennan's Reply." *Foreign Service Journal* 40 (Feb. 1963): 56-57.

Kennan defends his earlier statements criticizing the burgeoning bureaucracy in the State Dept., but admits himself "chastened" by his experience in Yugoslavia, where he did not move to reduce the staff of the embassy.

232. "Pasternak Collaborator's Arrest." *New York Times,* 26 Jan. 1963, 28.

Deplores the arrest and imprisonment of a literary collaborator of Boris Pasternak, and comments that it is not in keeping with the image of the Soviet Union that Khrushchev is trying to project.

TRANSLATIONS

233. *Dongseo Woegyo Bisa.* Translated by Gyujeong Kim. Seoul: Bagmunsa, 1963. 424p.

(Not seen. Tr. of the 1961 work *Russia and the West under Lenin and Stalin,* no. **206.**)

234. *Soryeon-gwa Wonjaryeog-gwa Seobang.* Translated by Jeong-dong Yeo. Seoul: Beobmunsa, 1963. 134p.

(Not seen. Tr. of the 1958 work *Russia, the Atom and the West,* no. **136.**)

235. *World Technology and Human Destiny.* Edited by Raymond Aron, translated by Richard Seaver. Ann Arbor, Mich.: Univ. of Michigan Press, 1963. vi, 246p.

A collection of papers and transcripts of discussions at a conference at Rheinfelden in 1959. Kennan's contributions (pp. 75-79, 122-124, 182-185) are brief statements which address Soviet totalitarianism, changes in Soviet society, and effects of the Cold War, problems of modern industrial society, population growth and the environment, and the value of Western institutions as examples to Third World countries.

(Tr. of the 1960 work *Colloques de Rheinfelden,* no. **185**. Also translated no. **214**. Excerpts reprinted nos. **320,402.**)

REPRINTS

236. *American Diplomacy, 1900-1950.* New York: New American Library, 1963. 127p. (Charles R. Walgreen Foundation Lectures.)
(Not seen. Another ed. of the 1951 work, no. **22**.)

237. "America's Administrative Response." Parts 1-3. *Foreign Service Journal* 40 (Aug./Sept./Oct. 1963): 23-26, 22-26, 26-27.
(Reprint of the 1958 article, no. **140**.)

238. "The Confusion of Ends and Means." In *The Soviet Crucible*, 2d ed., edited by Samuel Hendel, 635-639. Princeton, N.J.: Van Nostrand, 1963.
(Excerpt from the 1963 work *World Technology and Human Destiny*, no. **235**. Reprinted nos. **320,402**. For the original, see no. **185**.)

239. "Foreign Policy and Christian Conscience." In *Contemporary Moral Issues*, edited by Harry K. Girvetz, 9-17. Belmont, Calif.: Wadsworth Pub. Co., 1963.
(Abridgement of the 1959 article, no. **167**.)

240. "World War II." In *The Making of American History*, vol. 2, 3d ed., edited by Donald Sheehan, 476-490. New York: Holt, Rinehart & Winston, 1963.
(Reprint of the 1954 excerpt no. **86**.)

1964

BOOKS

241. *On Dealing with the Communist World.* New York: Published for the Council on Foreign Relations by Harper & Row, 1964. xi, 57p. (Elihu Root Lectures, 1963/1964.)
Three lectures, "The Rationale of Coexistence," "East-West Trade," and "Polycentrism and Western Policy," in which Kennan advocates a less rigid policy on the part of the U.S. towards the Soviet Union, is critical of "liberationist" rhetoric and of economic, political, and military policies which solidify the division of Europe. (Reprinted no. **281**. See also the 1964 article no. **246**. Excerpts reprinted nos. **254,265,277,321**. Translated nos. **272-273**. Translated excerpt, nos. **250,271**.)

ARTICLES

242. "A Fresh Look at Our China Policy." *New York Times Magazine*, 22 Nov. 1964, 27+.
Kennan is not sanguine about bettering relations with the Chinese; they are aggressive and xenophobic. But containment, rather than liberation, of Communist China is still the best course. The U.S. could do more to open doors to negotiation, beginning with diplomatic recognition. Containment in Southeast Asia should be supported--neither withdrawal nor escalation will help the situation there.
(Reprinted no. **295**.)

243. "Japanese Security and American Policy." *Foreign Affairs* 43 (Oct. 1964): 14-28.
Some assumptions behind existing agreements on Japanese security are no longer valid; some changes are in order. Strictures against Japan maintaining a large

military, coupled with continuing sources of conflict in the area, make better relations with Communist China and the Soviet Union desirable. Japanese and U.S. policies need not be identical.

244. "K's Exit Easy to Exaggerate." *Washington Post*, 18 Oct. 1964, sec. E, 1.
Khrushchev's retirement signals a turning point but not a major policy change. It was necessary for healing the rifts in the Communist parties. It is a triumph for Mao, but a complete rapprochement between Moscow and Peking is unlikely, and the U.S. can expect increased hostility toward the capitalist West. Kennan comments that succession in Soviet government has once again taken place without a crisis.
(See also "A Triumph for Mao," no. **248**.)

245. "Moving Towards War, 1914: What Happened in Russia." *The Listener* 72 (July 9, 1964): 47-50.
Some domestic reforms were attempted in Russia before the Revolution, but parliamentary government was weak and the foreign policies of the ruling elite did not provide the peace needed for reforms to advance. The alliance with France and the war with Japan were damaging.

246. "Polycentrism and Western Policy." *Foreign Affairs* 42 (Jan. 1964): 171-183.
Kennan advocates less rigid policies toward the satellite countries and recognition of polycentric tendencies in the Communist world. A policy which ignores these tendencies could face the satellites with a choice between either tightening ties with the Communist bloc or violent wars of liberation. (Reprinted 1964 in *On Dealing With the Communist World*, no. **241**. Translated no. **250**.)

247. "The Price We Paid for War." *Atlantic*, Oct. 1964, 50-54.
Views the causes and aftermath of World War I. The results of the war were unanticipated and damaging to the international structure in Europe: instability in Eastern Europe, the Russian Revolution, and destruction of the German Empire. Even before the development of the nuclear weapon, major war was not viable "as an instrument of policy."

248. "A Triumph for Mao." *The Times* (London), 18 Oct. 1964, 13.
(See "K's Exit Easy to Exaggerate," no. **244**, for annotation.)

BOOK REVIEWS

249. Review of *The British "Intervention" in Transcaspia, 1918-1919*, by C.H. Ellis. *Slavic Review* 23 (June 1964): 347-348.

TRANSLATIONS

250. "Fragen an den Westen. Was die Differenzierung im Ostblock für uns bedeutet." *Die Zeit*, 10 Apr. 1964, 8.
(Tr. of the 1964 article, "Polycentrism and Western Policy" no. **246**. See also no. **241**.)

251. *Kyosan Sekai To Do Tsukiau Ka: Shinjidai No Tozai Kenkei*. Translated by Takahashi Tadashi. Tokyo: Dobundo, 1964. 142p.

(Not seen. Tr. of the 1964 work, *On Dealing with the Communist World*, no. **241**.)

REPRINTS

252. *American Diplomacy, 1900-1950*. New York: New American Library, 1964. 127p. (Charles R. Walgreen Foundation Lectures.)
(Another ed. of the 1951 work, no. **22**)

253. "Contemporary Perspectives." In *Russian Foreign Policy: Essays in Historical Perspective*, edited by Ivo J. Lederer, 595-601. New Haven: Yale Univ. Press, 1964.
(Reprint of the 1962 article, no. **220**.)

254. "Diplomacy in the Age of the Thaw." *The Observer*, 14 June 1964, 11.
(Excerpt from the 1964 work *On Dealing With the Communist World*, no. **241**.)

255. "Foreign Policy and Christian Conscience." In *Contemporary Moral Issues*, edited by Harry K. Girvetz, 9-17. Belmont, Calif.: Wasdworth, 1964.
(Abridgement of the 1959 article, no. **167**.)

256. "George F. Kennan's Observations on the New Soviet Leadership, August 1956." In *Ideas and Diplomacy*, edited by Norman A. Graebner, 823-829. New York: Oxford Univ. Press, 1964.
(Abridgement of the 1956 article "Overdue Changes in Our Foreign Policy," no. **104**.)

257. "It's History But Is It Literature?" In *Opinions and Perspectives from the New York Times Book Review*, edited and with an introd. by Francis Brown, 386-394. Boston: Houghton Mifflin, 1964.
(Reprint of the 1959 article, no. **169**.)

258. "The Realist Position." In *America's Entry Into World War I*, edited by Herbert J. Bass, 102-108. New York: Holt, Rinehart and Winston, 1964.
(Excerpt from the 1951 work *American Diplomacy, 1900-1950*, no. **22**.)

259. "Totalitarianism in the Modern World." In *Totalitarianism*, edited by Carl J. Friedrich, 17-36. New York: Grosset and Dunlap, 1964.
(Reprint of the 1954 article, no. **80**.)

260. "We Have Seen Our Public Life Debauched." In *Ideas and Diplomacy*, edited by Norman A. Graebner, 768-771. New York: Oxford Univ. Press, 1964.
(Abridgement of the 1954 article "The Illusion of Security," no. **76**.)

1965

ARTICLES

261. "An Authority on Communism Says We're Letting this One Area Disbalance Whole Policy." *Washington Post*, 12 Dec. 1965, sec. E, 1, 4.
The war in Southeast Asia is preventing initiatives for improving relations with the Soviet Union and finding solutions for other problems such as nuclear disarmament and a divided Germany. Negotiations at this time may not be useful, but should aim

to "cool off" the conflict.

262. "A Case for Sparing the Spurs: Forcing Russia's Hand on Big Issues Could Push Kremlin into Siding with China on Viet-Nam." *Washington Post*, 7 Mar. 1965, sec. E, 4.

An analysis of policy alternatives in the face of the Sino-Soviet conflict. The U.S. is overlooking the strategic advantages of improving relations with the Soviets. We need to look to areas where agreements can be had, such as nuclear disarmament and Germany, and avoid conflict in the struggles in developing countries, of which Vietnam is an example. A continuing Russian-Chinese rivalry makes the development of "Titoist tendencies" in these situations more likely.
(Reprinted In "Statement of George F. Kennan." *Report on the Sino-Soviet Conflict*, no. **266**.)
[From the Walter E. Edge Lecture, Princeton University.]

263. "The Ethics of Anti-Communism." *University: A Princeton Quarterly* 24 (spring 1965): 3-5.

Communism is not monolithic, and our struggle with communists is not a manichean one of good and evil. The term "anti-communism" is vague and the sentiment dangerous in obscuring our real problems and diverting energies which could be better spent finding solutions to pressing needs of society.
(Reprinted no. **284**.)

264. [Statement]. In *On Coexistence*, 13-16. Santa Barbara, Calif.: Center for the Study of Democratic Institutions, 1965. (Occasional Paper Resulting from an International Convocation on the Requirements of Peace.)

Kennan details "sterile and unsatisfactory" aspects of Western policy: assumption of the Soviet desire to attack, reliance on the nuclear deterrent, pressure for a united Germany within the Atlantic Pact, and for economic and political ties in Western Europe to the exclusion of the East, and recommends changes. Followed by a discussion, pp. 24-26.
(Reprinted nos. **278-279,292**.)

DOCUMENTS

265. "Statement of Dr. George F. Kennan." In U.S. Congress. Senate. Committee on Foreign Relations. *East-West Trade*. Hearings, 89th Cong., 1st sess. Pt.2, Feb. 24- 26, 1965, 147-159. Washington, D.C.: GPO, 1965. (Y4F76/2:T67/965/pt.2)

Normal trade with the Communist countries of Eastern Europe is useful, and the U.S. should pursue trade more vigorously. However, Kennan does not recommend aid programs or long-term credit. (Contains a reprint of the chapter "East-West Trade" in *On Dealing With the Communist World* no. **241**, pp. 153-159.)

266. "Statement of George F. Kennan." In U.S. Congress. House. Committee on Foreign Affairs. Subcommittee on the Far East and the Pacific. *Report on the Sino-Soviet Conflict and Its Implications*. Hearings, 89th Cong., 1st sess. Mar. 10-11, 15-18, 23, and 31, 1965, 48-49. Washington, D.C.: GPO, 1965. (Y4F76/1:Si6)

In his testimony, Kennan says the U.S. is militarily overextended, and the dangers of communist aggression are exaggerated. He outlines some of the more independent policies among the communist countries, and mentions his disagreement with the implementation of the Truman Doctrine. He would like to see withdrawal

from Vietnam, without political damage to the U.S. or to world peace. Kennan advises more normal relations with mainland China, and he advises against exacerbation of the Sino-Soviet conflict. (Contains a reprint of "A Case for Sparing the Spurs," no. **262**, pp. 76-79.
(Reprinted nos. **275-276,317**.)

COMMENTARIES

267. "China." Letter to the editor. *The Correspondent*, winter 1965, 94-95.
Responding to a book review essay Kennan expresses his view that he sees no hopeful outcome for U.S.-Chinese relations. It would be a mistake for the U.S. to give up the influence it has in Southeast Asia to the Chinese.

268. "Introduction." In *Power and the Soviet Elite: "The Letter of an Old Bolshevik" and Other Essays*, by Boris I. Nicolaevsky, edited by Janet D. Zagoria, xiii-xxi. New York: Published for the Hoover Institution on War, Revolution and Peace by Praeger, 1965. (Hoover Institution Publication, 52/6.)
Kennan describes conditions for the establishment of "personal terrorism" under Stalin.
(Reprinted no. **296**.)

269. "Kennan States View on Soviet Relations." Letter to the editor. *New York Times*, 30 Mar. 1965, 46.
Kennan takes issue with critics who view his approach to better relations with the Soviets as one-sided. He has always maintained that the Soviets will also have to make compromises, but sees opportunities for initiatives that the U.S. has ignored.

270. "A Policy for the Far East: An Exchange." With A. J. Muste. *Liberation*, Apr. 1965, 6-11, 24.
Kennan replies briefly, yielding little, to Muste's criticisms of "A Fresh Look at Our China Policy" (no. **242**), in which Kennan argues that the U.S. must see its commitment in Vietnam through and not yield the area to the Chinese Communists.

TRANSLATIONS

271. "Der Ost-West Handel." *Der Monat* 17 (1964/1965): 13-39.
(Not seen. Tr. excerpt from the 1964 work *On Dealing with the Communist World*, no. **241**.)

272. *Sameksistems med den Kommunistiske Verden*. Translated by Erling Welblund. Copenhagen: Fremad, 1965. 63p.
(Not seen. Tr. of the 1964 work *On Dealing with the Communist World*, no. **241**.)

273. *Vom Ungang mit der Kommunistischen Welt*. Translated by Otto Baumhauer. Stuttgart: Steingruben Verlag, 1965. 75p.
(Not seen. Tr. of the 1964 work *On Dealing with the Communist World*, no. **241**.)

REPRINTS

274. *American Diplomacy, 1900-1950*. Chicago, University of Chicago Press, 1965. ix,

154p. (Charles R. Walgreen Foundation Lectures.)
(Not seen. Another ed. of the 1951 work, no. **22**.)

275. "American Involvement." In *The Viet-Nam Reader*, edited by Marcus G. Raskin and Bernard B. Fall, 15-31. New York: Random House, 1965.
(Reprint of the 1965 Document "Statement of George F. Kennan," no. **266**.)

276. ______. In *The Vietnam Reader*, edited by Marcus G. Raskin and Bernard B. Fall, 15-31. New York: Vintage, 1965.
(Reprint of the 1965 Document "Statement of George F. Kennan," no. **266**.)

277. "East-West Trade." In U.S. Congress. Senate. Committee on Foreign Relations. *East-West Trade*. Hearings. Pt. 2, Feb. 24-26, 1965, 153-159. Washington, D.C.: GPO, 1965.
(Excerpt reprinted from the 1964 work *On Dealing With the Communist World*, no. **241**. For Hearing annotation, see no. **265**.)

278. "A European Settlement." In *Peace on Earth, Pacem In Terris*, edited by Edward Reed, 77-83. New York: Pocket Books, 1965.
(Reprint from the 1965 work *On Coexistence*, no. **264**.)

279. "Kennan Reviews Foreign Policy in Light of *Pacem*." *National Catholic Reporter*, Mar. 3, 1965, 5.
(Reprint from the 1965 work *On Coexistence*, no. **264**.)

280. "The Military Problem." In *America's Foreign Policy*, rev. ed., edited with an introduction and notes by Harold Karan Jacobson, 435-440. New York: Random House, 1965.
(Reprint of the 1960 excerpt, no. **199**.)

281. *On Dealing with the Communist World.* New York: Published for the Council on Foreign Relations by Harper & Row, 1965. xi, 59p. (Elihu Root Lectures, 1963/64.)
(Not seen. Another ed. of the 1964 work no. **241**.)

282. "The Problem of Eastern and Central Europe." In *America's Foreign Policy*, rev. ed., edited with an introduction and notes by Harold Karan Jacobson, 425-435. New York: Random House, 1965.
(Reprint of the 1960 excerpt no. **201**.)

283. "The Sources of Soviet Conduct." In *America's Foreign Policy*, rev. ed., edited with an introduction and notes by Harold Karan Jacobson, 254-270. New York: Random House, 1965.
(Reprint of the 1960 reprint no. **203**.)

284. "There Is a Right Way to Counter Communism." *Fellowship*, Nov. 1965, 5-7.
(Reprint of the 1965 article, "The Ethics of Anti-Communism, no. **263**.)

285. "Two Planes of International Reality." In *Issues in American Diplomacy*, vol. 1, edited by Armin Rappaport, 3-15. New York: Macmillan, 1965.
(Excerpt from the 1954 work *Realities of American Foreign Policy*, no. **70**. Reprinted no. **303**.)

1966

ARTICLES

286. "Europe in East-West Relations." *Survey* 58 (Jan. 1966): 118-127.

Reviews the tenuous stability of a divided Europe and problems leading to the division: the place of a united Germany, and acceptable borders for new states resulting from the breakup of the Austro-Hungarian Empire. These problems have not been solved; there would be hope for their resolution in some kind of European federation overcoming national sovereignty. Progress has been made toward this end in the West, and Kennan sees possibilities for East-West agreements.

[Adapted from a lecture at the "European Talks" in Vienna, summer 1965.]

287. "Die Illusion vom schnellen Frieden. Bemerkungen zur Amerikanischen Vietnam-Politik," *Die Zeit*, 18 Jan. 1966, 3.

A communist victory in Vietnam would create a police state, but the framing of U.S. policy in terms of defending democracy is ahistorical and unrealistic. The U.S. commitment in Vietnam is detrimental to other policies in its interest, such as improving relations with the Soviets, disarmament, and the work of the U.N. The U.S. needs to distinguish between long-term and short-term interests.

288. "Why Do I Hope?" *University: A Princeton Quarterly* 29 (summer 1966): 3-5.

Pessimistic about the state of American culture and the future of the world, Kennan nevertheless finds loving relationships and human responsibility reasons for hopeful optimism.

[Sermon at Princeton University Chapel, Feb. 1966.]

DOCUMENTS

288a. "Russia--Seven Years Later." In *Foreign Relations of the United States, 1944*, vol. 4, 902-914. Washington, D.C.: GPO, 1966. (S1.1)

Extracts from a memorandum written in Sept. 1944, when Kennan was Counselor in the embassy in Moscow, warning that contradictions and conflicts in Russian civilization will make it difficult, if not impossible for an American to understand. He outlines Soviet foreign policy, domestic and intellectual life, characterizes Soviet leadership, and emphasizes Soviet territorial ambitions for empire in Eastern Europe. The Soviet goal is power; communism is a secondary concern.

(Reprinted in Kennan's *Memoirs, 1925-1950*, no. **306**.)

289. "Statement of Hon. George Kennan." In U.S. Congress. Senate. Committee on Foreign Relations. *Supplemental Foreign Assistance Fiscal Year 1966--Vietnam*. Hearings before the Committee on Foreign Relations United States Senate, 89th Cong., 2d sess. Pt. 1. Jan. 28, Feb. 4, 8, 10, 17-18, 1966, 331-394. Washington, D.C.: GPO, 1966. (Y4F76/2:V67/8/pt.1)

Vietnam is not a vital interest, and the U.S. should not be involved to the extent that it is. Kennan advises extrication from Vietnam, is in agreement with General Gavin's defense of enclaves, and warns against trying to solve the internal political problems of other countries. With a question and answer exchange.

(Reprinted nos. **297-299,302,305**.)

COMMENTARIES

290. "Boris Ivanovich Nicolaevsky, 1887-1966." *Slavic Review* 25 (June 1966): 375-377.
Kennan, in this memorial tribute, takes the occasion to comment on Americans' imperfect understanding of the Russian people, and to recognize the contributions of B. I. Nicolaevsky to better understanding between the two peoples. (Nicolaevsky was a defector from the Soviet Union who had revealed details of the struggle within the Communist Party leading to the purges of the 1930's in his controversial "Letter of An Old Bolshevik.")

291. "Kennan Urges War Policy of Moderation." Letter to the editor. *New York Times*, 25 Sept. 1966, sec. 4, 11.
Strategic bombing in Vietnam has not had its intended effect, has caused immense suffering of the Vietnamese people, and instability in international relations. It is time for a change of policy.

TRANSLATIONS

291a. *Rusya Tatakhalla 'An Al-Harb*. Translated by 'Adil Shafiq. Cairo: al-Dar al-Qawmiyah, 1966. 464p.
(Not seen. Tr. of the 1956 work *Soviet American Relations, 1917-1920*. Vol. 1, *Russia Leaves the War*., no. **97**.)

REPRINTS

292. "Contribution to the Discussion of European Problems at Pacem In Terris Convocation." In *Peace Is Possible*, edited by Elizabeth Jay Hollins, 289-93. New York: Grossman Publ., 1966.
(Reprint of 1965 "[Statement]" in *On Coexistence*, no. **264**.)

293. "The Decision on Siberia." In *Issues in American Diplomacy*, vol. 2, edited by Armin Rappaport, 187-199. New York: Macmillan, 1966.
(Excerpt from the 1958 work *Soviet-American Relations 1917-1920*. Vol. 2, *The Decision to Intervene*, no. **138**.)

294. "The Experience of Writing History." In *The Craft of American History*, vol. 2, edited by A. S. Eisenstadt, 270-278. New York: Harper & Row, 1966.
(Reprint of the 1960 article, no. **188**.)

295. "A Fresh Look at Our China Policy." In U.S. Congress. Senate. Committee on Foreign Relations. *Supplemental Foreign Assistance Fiscal Year 1966--Vietnam*. Hearings before the Committee on Foreign Relations, United States Senate, 89th Cong., 2d sess. Pt. 1. Jan. 28, Feb. 4, 8, 10, 17-18, 1966, 394-399. Washington, D.C.: GPO, 1966.
(Reprint of the 1964 article, no. **242**.)

296. "Introduction." In *Power and the Soviet Elite: "The Letter of an Old Bolshevik," and Other Essays*, by Boris I. Nicolaevsky, edited by Janet Zagoria, xiii-xxi. London: Pall Mall, 1966.
(Not seen. Another ed. of the 1965 commentary, no. **268**.)

297. "Is American Intervention Justifiable?" In *China, Vietnam, and the United States, Highlights of the Hearings of the Senate Foreign Relations Committee*, 195-202. Washington, D.C.: Public Affairs Press, 1966.
(Reprint of 1966 "Statement of Hon. George Kennan," no. **289**.)

298. "Kennan on Vietnam." *New Republic*, 26 Feb. 1966, 18-30.
(Reprint of 1966 "Statement of Hon. George Kennan," no. **289**.)

299. "Kennan Statement." *Congressional Quarterly Weekly Report* 24 (18 Feb. 1966): 431-432.
(Reprint of 1966 "Statement of Hon. George Kennan," no. **289**.)

300. *The Realities of American Foreign Policy*. New York: Norton, 1966. ix, 119p.
(Another ed. of the 1954 work, no. **70**, with a new preface.)

301. "The Sisson Documents." In *Agents of Deceit: Frauds, Forgeries, and Political Intrigue Among Nations*, by Paul W. Blackstock, with an appendix by George F. Kennan, 247-276. Chicago: Quadrangle Books, 1966.
(Reprint of the 1956 article, no. **105**.)

302. "A Statement on Vietnam." In *Representative American Speeches, 1965/1966*, 56-65. New York: H. W. Wilson Co., 1966.
(Reprint of the 1966 document "Statement of Hon. George Kennan," no. **289**.)

303. "The Two Planes of International Reality." In *The Puritan Ethic in United States Foreign Policy*, edited by David L. Larson, 25-42. New York: Van Nostrand, 1966.
(Reprint of the 1965 reprint no. **285**.)

304. "The Vietnam Debate." *Survival*, Apr. 1966, 108-111.
(Reprint of the 1966 document "Statement of Hon. George Kennan," no. **289**.)

305. "Vietnam Policy--Testimony at the Committee Hearings." *Congressional Digest* 45: (Apr. 1966): 108-110.
(Excerpt from the 1966 document "Statement of Hon. George Kennan," no. **289**.)

1967

BOOKS

306. *Memoirs, 1925-1950*. Boston: Little, Brown, 1967. 583p.
In this first volume of memoirs, the primary focus is Kennan's view of his role in policy-making in major decisions in the postwar years. He discusses the Long Telegram, the "X" article (no. **2**), revealing his agreement with many of Lippmann's criticisms at the time, his reaction to the Truman Doctrine, development of the Marshall Plan and NATO, and his analysis of the occupation in Japan. Appended are essays written by Kennan in the mid-1940s analyzing Soviet objectives and characteristics: "Russia--Seven Years Later" (also published in *FRUS* 1944, v. 4, see no. **288a**), "Russia's International Position at the Close of the War with Germany," "Telegraphic Message From Moscow of Feb. 22, 1946," (full text in *FRUS* 1946 v. 6, no. **350**), and "The United States and Russia."
(Reprinted nos. **344,356,522**. Excerpts reprinted no. **390a**. See also v.2, no. **380**.)

ARTICLES

307. "Causes of the Russian Revolution." *The Listener* 78 (2 Nov. 1967): 557-560.
(An abridgement of a lecture published in *Revolutionary Russia*, 1968, as "The Breakdown of the Tsarist Autocracy in Revolutionary Russia," no. **330**. See for annotation.)

308. "Meet the Press: Guest Prof. George F. Kennan." Television and radio interview by Lawrence E. Spivak, Max Frankel, Elie Abel and Carl T. Rowan, Nov. 5, 1967. Washington, D.C.: Merkle Press, 1967. 11p. (*Meet the Press*, v.11, no. 45.)
Kennan notes technological accomplishments of the Soviets, also the great human cost of these achievements. Soviet policy has become less expansionist. "Containment" in Vietnam is a misuse of the principle. Kennan also talks about policy towards China, and the limitations of democracy in conducting foreign policy.

309. "The Quest for Concept." *Harvard Today*, autumn, 1967, 11-17.
Kennan outlines his objections to the legalism and moralism that characterized foreign policy thinking in the late 19th and early 20th centuries. These persisting attitudes led postwar policy-makers to reduce containment to a purely military and strategic policy, with the Vietnam war as a mistaken consequence. Democracy makes it difficult to ground foreign policy in realistic national interests and limitations.
[From an address at Harvard University, spring 1967.]

310. "The Russian Revolution--Fifty Years After: Its Nature and Consequences." *Foreign Affairs* 46 (Oct. 1967): 1-21.
Analyzes the historical significance of the Russian Revolution in hastening the demise of the European colonial system, in the political polarization of the West and of international discourse, and internally in the achievement--and high cost--of industrialization.

DOCUMENTS

311. U.S. Congress. Senate. Committee on Foreign Relations. *The Communist World in 1967.* Hearings . . . 90th Cong. 1st sess., with former Ambassador to the Soviet Union and Yugoslavia, George F. Kennan, Jan. 30, 1967. Washington, D.C.: GPO, 1967. iii, 68p. (Y4F76/2:C73/5/1961)
A wide-ranging discussion on political and economic conditions in the Soviet Union, Eastern Europe, and China and on the Soviets' role in the Vietnam war. Kennan sees "disunity" in the Communist bloc and openings for bettering relations, of which the U.S. has not taken advantage.
(Reprinted no. **325**.)

COMMENTARIES

312. "Question of a September 1936 Plenum of the CPSU Central Committee." [An exchange by Abdurakhman Avtorkhanov, John A. Armstrong, Robert M. Slusser, and George F. Kennan.] *Slavic Review* 26 (Dec. 1967): 665-677.
Includes a letter to Slusser in which Kennan clarifies his position on the question under discussion. He concludes there is no hard evidence for a plenum, only for high-level meetings.

313. ["Remarks."] In *Three Tributes to J. Robert Oppenheimer*, by Hans A. Bethe, Henry DeWolf Smyth, and George Kennan, 27-30. Princeton, N.J.: Institute for Advanced Study, 1967.

Kennan's tribute to his friend and colleague at the Institute for Advanced Study. (Reprinted no. **322.**)

314. "Text of Kennan's Statement on the Role He Played." *New York Times*, 22 Apr. 1967, 11.

Describes advice he gave to Svetlana Alliluyeva (Stalin's daughter) on her decision to come to the U.S.

TRANSLATIONS

315. "Fünfzig Jahre nach dem Sturm: Welche Veränderungen hat die sowjetische Revolution bewirkt?" *Die Zeit*, 17 Oct. 1967, 8.

(Tr. of the last part of the 1967 article "The Russian Revolution--Fifty Years After," no. **310**. See also no. **316**.)

316. "Das russische Erdbeben. Warum die Bolschewisten die Revolution zum Erfolg führen könnten." *Die Zeit*, 10 Oct. 1967, 8.

(Tr. of the first part of the 1967 article "The Russian Revolution--Fifty Years After," no. **310**. See also no. **315**.)

REPRINTS

317. "American Involvement." In *The Viet-Nam Reader*, rev. ed., edited by Marcus G. Raskin and Bernard B. Fall, 15-31. New York: Random House, 1967.

(Reprint of the 1965 reprint, no. **275**. Original from "Statement of George F. Kennan," no. **266**.)

318. ______. In *The Viet-Nam Reader*, rev. ed., edited by Marcus G. Raskin and Bernard B. Fall, 15-31. New York: Vintage Books, 1967.

(See no. **317**.)

319. "The Case for a Containment Policy." In *Containment and the Origins of the Cold War*, edited by Edwin C. Rozwenc and Kenneth Lindfors, 18-26. Boston: D. C. Heath & Co., 1967.

(Abridgement of the 1947 article "The Sources of Soviet Conduct," no. **2**.)

320. "The Confusion of Ends and Means." In *The Soviet Crucible*, 3d ed., edited by Samuel Hendel, 401-403. Princeton, N.J.: Van Nostrand, 1967.

(Excerpt from the 1963 translation *World Technology and Human Destiny*, no. **235**. Original no. **185**.)

321. "On Dealing with the Communist World." In *Essays in American Diplomacy*, edited by Armin Rappaport, 312-331. New York: Macmillan, 1967.

(Reprint of two of the lectures from the 1964 work, no. **241**.)

322. "Oppenheimer." *Encounter*, Apr. 1967, 55-56.

(Reprint of the 1967 commentary "Remarks," no. **313**.)

323. *Soviet-American Relations, 1917-1920.* Vol. 1, *Russia Leaves the War.* New York: Atheneum, 1967. xiii, 544p.
(Not seen. Another ed of the 1956 work, no. **97.**)

324. ______. Vol. 2, *The Decision to Intervene.* New York: Atheneum, 1967. xii, 513p.
(Not seen. Another ed. of the 1958 work, no. **138.**)

325. "U.S. Policy in Asia--As Two Ex-Envoys See It." *U.S. News & World Report,* 13 Feb. 1967, 19-20.
(Excerpt from the 1967 document *The Communist World in 1967,* no. **311.**)

1968

BOOKS

326. *Democracy and the Student Left.* By George F. Kennan and students and teachers from Barnard, Brandeis, Brooklyn . . . . Boston: Little, Brown, 1968. xi, 239p.
Contains the text of "Rebels Without a Program," (see no. **334**) critical comments from students and faculty at various institutions, plus a reply by Kennan.

327. ______. London: Hutchinson, 1968. [11], 239p.
(Not seen.)

328. ______. New York: Bantam Books, 1968. 208p.
(Not seen.)

329. *From Prague After Munich: Diplomatic Papers, 1938-1940.* Princeton, N.J.: Princeton Univ. Press, 1968. xxviii, 266p.
Letters and papers written when Kennan was Secretary of the legation in Prague, relating his observations of the German occupation in Czechoslavkia and illustrating "the dilemma of a limited collaboration with evil in the interests of its ultimate mitigation."

ARTICLES

330. "The Breakdown of the Tsarist Autocracy." In *Revolutionary Russia,* edited by Richard Pipes, 1-15. Cambridge, Mass.: Harvard Univ. Press, 1968.
Kennan argues that weaknesses in the autocratic regime, such as failure to establish parliamentary government, extreme nationalism, and the personality of Nicholas II, were more important in bringing about the Russian Revolution than the activities of the Bolsheviks. World War I was a decisive, but not a necessary factor in the breakdown of the autocracy.
(See also the 1967 article "Causes of the Russian Revolution," no. **307.**)

331. "Excerpts from a Draft Letter Written at Some Time During the First Months of 1945." *Slavic Review* 27 (Sept. 1968): 481-484.
A document written by Kennan in 1945, when he was Minister-Counselor in Moscow, in which he suggests that Stalin's power is not absolute, and mentions Beria and Malenkov as having a strong influence, particularly in internal affairs.

332. "Introducing Eugene McCarthy." *New York Review of Books,* 11 Apr. 1968, 14-16.

Kennan characterizes McCarthy as the candidate for those who disapprove of the war in Vietnam and want to see it end as soon as possible, and he details all that is wrong with the Administration's policy.

333. "The Legacy of Stalinism." *Proceedings of the Massachusetts Historical Society* 79 (1967): 123-134.
Reviews the effects of Stalinism in the Soviet Union, China, Eastern Europe, and the U.S. Kennan advocates realism in U.S. policy. Stalin is dead, but the U.S. still seems to be fighting Stalinism and fails to recognize polycentric tendencies in the communist countries.
[An address delivered to the society Apr. 21, 1967.]

334. "Rebels Without a Program." *New York Times Magazine*, 21 Jan. 1968, 22-23+.
A vigorous criticism of the rebellious youth of America. Kennan criticizes the radical left on college campuses for their militance, intolerance, and lack of reflective study; he takes aim at "hippies" for not recognizing that self-fulfillment and freedom comes through effort and self-restraint.
[Adapted from a speech at Swarthmore College.]
(See also the 1968 work *Democracy and the Student Left*, no. **326**. Reprinted no. **357**. Translated nos. **340-341**.)

335. "The Soviet Union, 1917-1939." In *The New Cambridge Modern History*. Vol. 12, *The Shifting Balance of World Forces, 1898-1945*, 2d ed., 433-472. Cambridge: Cambridge Univ. Press, 1968.
A summary history from the October Revolution to the Non-Aggression Pact with Germany, covering internal politics and foreign policy. In summing up this period, Kennan points to the negative effects of collectivization on agricultural output, while advances were made in industrialization. There were improvements in the educational system, but cultural life was stifled. Marxist-Leninist ideology became stultified.

PAMPHLETS

336. *America After Vietnam. An Address by the Honorable George F. Kennan on the Occasion of the Celebration of the Prelude to Independence at the Eighteenth-Century Capitol, Williamsburg, Virginia, June 1, 1968*. Williamsburg, Va.: Colonial Williamsburg, 1968. 24p.
American society is in disarray and out of touch with the principles of its founders. There are historical reasons for the rebellions of students and Negroes, demonstrations against the Vietnam war, and urban decay. More attention needs to be paid to domestic problems, and less to "extravagant excursions" abroad.
(Reprinted no. **343**.)

COMMENTARIES

337. "Preface." In *Decisions for a Decade*, by Edward M. Kennedy, 11-15. Garden City, N.Y.: Doubleday, 1968.
America seems unwilling or unable to deal with the crises of modern-day life: alienation and demoralization of Negroes and students, urban blight, destruction

of the environment, the Vietnam involvement, problems with NATO, the Near East and Communist China, and the menace of nuclear proliferation. Kennan commends Kennedy for discussion of these problems and posing practical solutions.

BOOK REVIEWS

338. "The Purges Unpurged," review of *The Great Terror*, by Robert Conquest. *New York Times Book Review*, 27 Oct. 1968, 2-3.

A brief review of the first book-length study of the 1930's purges in the Soviet Union. Kennan mentions that more needs to be known about the background and Stalin's early career to understand this period, and points out that the Soviets have failed to confront the Party's responsibility for what took place.

339. Review of *The Young Stalin: The Early Years of an Elusive Revolutionary*, by Edward Ellis Smith. *American Historical Review* 74 (Oct. 1968): 230-232.

Commends the author for taking up a subject which has received too little attention, particularly the period from 1900-1913, for which there is evidence that Stalin was an informer for the Secret Police.

TRANSLATIONS

339a. *Memoiren Eines Diplomaten*. Translated by Heidi von Alten. Stuttgart: Goverts, 1968. 607p.

(Not seen. Tr. of the 1967 work *Memoirs, 1925-1950*, no. **306**.)

339b. *Rebellen ohne Programm*. Translated by Heide von Alten. Stuttgart: Goverts, 1968. 171p.

(Not seen. Tr. of the 1968 work *Democracy and the Student Left*, no. **326**.)

340. "Rebellen ohne Programm. Die radikale Linke an den Amerikanischen Universitäten." *Der Monat* 20, 235 (1968): 16-24.

(Not seen. Tr. of the 1968 article "Rebels Without a Program," no. **334**.)

341. "Rebellen ohne Programm." *Zeitschrift für Politik* 15, 3 (1968): 272-280.

(Not seen. Tr. of the 1968 article "Rebels Without a Program," no. **334**.)

REPRINTS

342. "Foreign Policy and Christian Conscience." In *Contemporary Moral Issues*, 2d ed., edited by Harry K. Girvetz, 9-17. Belmont, Calif.: Wadsworth Pub. Co., 1968.

(Reprint of the 1959 article, no. **167**.)

343. "A Liberal Looks at Violence in U.S. and Where It's Leading." *U.S. News & World Report*, 17 June 1968, 66-69.

(Excerpt from the 1968 pamphlet *America After Vietnam*, no. **336**.)

344. *Memoirs, 1925-1950*. London: Hutchinson, 1968. 583p.

(Not seen. Another ed. of the 1967 work, no. **306**.)

1969

ARTICLES

345. "Address by George F. Kennan, President of the Academy." *Proceedings of the American Academy of Arts and Letters and the National Institute of Arts and Letters*, 2d ser., 19 (1969): 29-31.

Introductory remarks for the annual proceedings. Kennan sees the role of the artist as expressing "insight" into the "human predicament" rather than being a political actor.

346. "The Contemporary Literary Scene in Russia." Panel discussion with G. F. Kennan, Babette Deutsch, John Cheever, Lillian Hellman and Stanley J. Kunitz. *Proceedings of the American Academy of Arts and Letters and the National Institute of Arts and Letters*, 2d ser., 19 (1969): 3-26.

Kennan mentions the great respect for writers in the Soviet Union, and their own feelings of responsibility. The rebellion among writers is not political--they consider themselves loyal Soviet citizens--but it is for freedom of expression. They want to be able to write about Soviet reality.

347. "The Relation of Religion to Government." *Princeton Seminary Bulletin*, winter 1969, 42-47.

Politics and religion are two distinct spheres. The individual in government can aspire to moral responses in daily activities, but the nature of government is necessarily imperfect. The role of the church is to minister to individuals, not to engage in politics.

348. "Kennan Urges Speedy Withdrawal," interview by Israel Shenker. *New York Times*, 10 Nov. 1969, 3.

Urges withdrawal from Vietnam, and rejects the charge of "isolationism."

349. "Weltkonflikte und Weltpolizisten." *Die Zeit*, 18 Nov. 1969, 63-66.

(Not seen.)

DOCUMENTS

350. "The Chargé in the Soviet Union (Kennan) to the Secretary of State, Feb. 22, 1946." In U.S. Dept. of State. *Foreign Relations of the United States, 1946*. Vol. 6, *Eastern Europe; The Soviet Union*, 696-709. Washington, D.C.: GPO, 1969. (S1.1)

Later known as the "Long Telegram," and released only in this edition of *FRUS*, this memorandum was widely circulated in the State Dept. and overseas embassies at the time it was written. Kennan outlines the background situation in the Soviet Union, and he analyzes Soviet behavior in light of Marxist ideology combined with the traditional insecurity and suspicion of Russian rulers. The Soviets see no community of interests with the West, are ready to exploit weaknesses there, are expansionist, particularly on their immediate borders, and will be opportunistic elsewhere in advancing their power and influence. Nevertheless Kennan believes problems can be overcome without resorting to military conflict, by attention to the problems in the U.S. itself, and by specific measures to strengthen Europe. (Reprinted nos. **450,598,629**. An excerpt appears in Kennan's *Memoirs, 1925-1950*, no. **306**.)

COMMENTARIES

351. "Justice for Davies." Letter to the editor. *New York Times*, 22 Jan. 1969, 46.
Takes the occasion of the restoration of security clearance for John Paton Davies, Jr. to remark on the excesses of McCarthyism.

BOOK REVIEWS

352. "Remembering for the Russians," review of *The Siege of Leningrad*, by Harrison Salisbury. *Times Literary Supplement*, 14 Aug. 1969, 894.

353. Review of *Vospominiia Sovetskogo Posla: Voina, 1939-1943*, by I. M. Maisky. *Slavic Review* 28 (Mar. 1969): 150-153.
An appreciative review of the third volume of the autobiography of the man who was Moscow's ambassador in London.

TRANSLATIONS

353a. *Demokratin Och de Radikala Studenterna*. Translated by Richard Matz. Stockholm: Pan/Norstedt, 1969. 199p.
(Not seen. Tr. of the 1968 work *Democracy and the Student Left*, no. **326**.)

353b. *Ribelli Senza Programma*. Translated by Lidia Magliano. Milan: Rizzoli, 1969. viii, 207p.
(Not seen. Tr. of the 1968 work *Democracy and the Student Left*, no. **326**.)

REPRINTS

354. *American Diplomacy, 1900-1950*. Collector's edition. Chicago: Univ. of Chicago Press, 1969. ix, 154p. (Charles R. Walgreen Foundation Lectures.)
(Not seen. Another ed. of the 1951 work, no. **22**.)

355. "American Troops in Russia: Aid for the Czecho-Slovaks?" In *American Intervention in the Russian Civil War*, edited with an introduction by Betty Miller Unterberger, 51-60. Lexington, Mass.: D. C. Heath, 1969.
(Excerpt from the 1959 article "American Troops in Russia: the True Record," no. **163**.)

356. *Memoirs, 1925-1950*. Toronto, New York: Bantam Books, 1969. x,623p.
(Not seen. Another ed. of the 1967 work, no. **306**.)

357. "Student Left: Rebels Without a Program." *Reader's Digest*, Jan. 1969, 79-83.
(Abridgement of the 1968 article "Rebels Without a Program," no. **334**.)

1970

ARTICLES

358. "Amerikas Rückzug auf sich selbst." *Die Zeit*, 13 Oct. 1970, 3.
An analysis of U.S.-European relations. Kennan sees the U.S. pulling back from its global commitments, while Europe takes a larger role in its own defense.

Brandt's "Ostpolitik" opens new relations with Eastern Europe. Kennan views Nixon as reluctantly entering into a policy of détente.

359. "An Interview With George F. Kennan," by John F. Campbell. *Foreign Service Journal* 47 (Aug. 1970): 18-23.

Compares the influence of the Foreign Service Officer in his early days to the present, and analyzes reforms in the Service. Kennan describes factors contributing to the successes in U.S. policy, 1947-1949, and talks about Secretary of State Marshall.

360. "More Controls Ahead," panel discussion with George F. Kennan, Martin Peretz, Lillian Hellmann, Sam Brown, Stanley Hoffmann, and Allard K. Lowenstein. In *The Endless Crisis: America in the Seventies*, edited by Francois Duchene, 82-97. New York: Simon and Schuster, 1970.

Kennan sees a lack of leadership, ingrained traditional outlooks, and an inadequate institutional structure at fault in America's attempts to deal with problems of race, labor unrest, the environment, and quality of life. The book is the record of a four-day international conference at Princeton, December, 1968.

361. "To Prevent a World Wasteland: A Proposal." *Foreign Affairs* 48 (Apr. 1970): 401-413.

Calls for an international effort on environmental conservation and proposes a joint body of experts from the industrialized nations to establish needs, which will be able to make decisions on purely conservational grounds.
(Reprinted no. **364**.)

COMMENTARIES

362. "Con III Is Not the Answer." *New York Times*, 28 Oct. 1970, 47.

Responding to articles by Charles A. Reich, Kennan says replacing the government with mass consciousness-raising is not enough to solve the problems before us. He suggests instead constitutional revision and regional governments.

TRANSLATIONS

362a. *Lenin, Stalin to Seiho Sekai*. Translated by Kawabata Sueto, et al. Tokyo: Miraisha, 1970. 275, 7p.

(Not seen. Tr. of the 1961 work *Russia and the West Under Lenin and Stalin*, no. **206**.)

362b. *Memoari, 1925-1950*. Translated by Omer Lakomica. Rijeka (Yugoslavia): Otokar Kersovani, 1970. 414p.

(Not seen. Tr. of the 1967 work *Memoirs, 1925-1950*, no. **306**.)

REPRINTS

363. *American Diplomacy, 1900-1950*. Chicago: Univ. of Chicago Press, 1970. ix, 154p. (Charles R. Walgreen Foundation Lectures.)

(Not seen. Another ed. of the 1951 work, no. **22**.)

364. "To Prevent A World Wasteland." *Bulletin of Peace Proposals* 3 (1970): 222.

(Abridgement of the 1970 article, no. **361**.)

1971

BOOKS

365. *The Marquis de Custine and His "Russia in 1839."* Princeton, N.J.: Princeton Univ. Press, 1971. xii, 145p.

Kennan's historical study of the 1843 book by the Marquis de Custine and the reaction to it. Kennan finds the work's depiction of 1839 Russia to be flawed although it contains resonances that shed light on totalitarianism in the Russia of Joseph Stalin.

(Reprinted no. **390**. Excerpt reprinted no. **375**.)

ARTICLES

366. "Arbitration and Conciliation in American Diplomacy." *Arbitration Journal* 26 (1971): 1-33.

A history of U.S. arbitration agreements from 1899 to World War II. Kennan analyzes reasons for American enthusiasm for arbitration in dealing with international affairs, in spite of its limited effect, and deplores the focus on such abstract concepts instead of diplomacy based on thoughtful appraisal of international realities. The paper was written in 1951-1952. In a contemporary Preface, Kennan sees the nuclear weapon as foreclosing major wars--other ways will have to be found to settle conflicts.

367. "The Arts in American Society." *Cultural Affairs*, May 1971, 1-5.

The arts are a necessary part of our culture, and need financial support, not just from commercial interests. Communication is needed beween the artist and the public, whose aesthetics are probably quite different.

368. "Hazardous Courses in Southern Africa." *Foreign Affairs* 49 (Jan. 1971): 218-236.

Kennan looks at frictions in Southern African countries, concentrating on South Africa. Although apartheid is "shocking and depressing," not all of South Africa's problems will be solved by its demise. He sees hope for internal change, and advises against economic pressure and international isolation. Regarding South West Africa, Angola, and Mozambique, he urges the West to adopt policies which will not lead to violence.

(Reprinted no. **379**.)

369. "The Historiography of the Early Political Career of Stalin." *Proceedings of the American Philosophical Society* 115 (June 1971): 165-169.

Sets forth reasons to believe that Stalin was probably an informer for the Tsarist police, and surmises that this influenced his behavior during the purges in the 1930s, and is a factor in the ban on inquiries into Stalin's life and the removal of his body from its place of honor in the Red Square Mausoleum.

370. "Report on Professor and Mrs. George F. Kennan's Visit to South Africa and South West Africa." In *South Africa: Three Visitors Report*, by George F. Kennan, Leon Gordenker, and Wilton Dillon, 5-18. Pasadena: Munger Africana Library, 1971. (Munger Africana Library Notes, no.2.)

Primarily a report on the itinerary and people met during a trip sponsored by the United States-South Africa Leader Exchange Program. Kennan calls the situation in South Africa tragic and complex. He is not against the bantustan concept, but is critical of policies that treat the presence of blacks in urban areas, such as Soweto, as a temporary phenomenon. There is much to be critical of in South Africa, but much of the criticism is ill-informed and self-righteous. Expanding, not limiting, contacts is the more hopeful course for change.

BOOK REVIEWS

371. "Dead Souls," review of *Khrushchev Remembers*, by N. S. Khrushchev. *New York Review of Books*, 25 Feb. 1971, 3-4.

Kennan questions the authenticity of this work and speculates that it was published to recover some of Khrushchev's more liberal ideas in the face of the greater restrictions of the Brezhnev regime.

COMMENTARIES

372. "Introduction." In *Russia*, rev. ed., by Charles W. Thayer, 7. New York: Time-Life Books, 1971.

Reviews the history of U.S.-Soviet relations; sees Soviet policy stemming from its position as a great power rather than from revolutionary ideology.

373. "A Note on Russian Foreign Policy." *Encounter*, Feb. 1971, 53-54.

Points to the difference in Soviet foreign policy between bordering countries, where it is more like internal policy, and other areas where foreign policy functions much as in any other nation. Kennan comments on a characteristic disinterest of the Russians in really getting to know about the Western way of life.

374. "Opening of the Ceremonies and Induction of New Members of the Academy." *Proceedings of the American Academy of Arts and Letters and the National Institute of Arts and Letters*, 2d ser., 21 (1971): 3-6.

Kennan holds out the hope that the arts can encourage mutual understanding in these times of great uncertainty.

REPRINTS

375. "Custine." *New Yorker*, May 1 1971, 46-93.

(Excerpt from the 1971 work *The Marquis de Custine and his "Russia in 1839"*, no. **365**.)

376. "Foreign Aid as a National Policy." *Proceedings of the Academy of Political Science* 30 (May 1971): 175-183.

(Reprint of the 1950 article "Foreign Aid In The Framework of National Policy," no. **8**.)

377. "Limitations of Economic Aid." In *Readings in American Foreign Policy*, 2d ed., rev., edited by Robert A. Goldwin, 593-596. New York: Oxford Univ. Press, 1971.

(Excerpt from the 1958 work *Russia, the Atom, and the West*, no. **136**.)

378. "The Sources of Soviet Conduct." In *Readings in American Foreign Policy*, 2d ed., rev., edited by Robert A. Goldwin, 337-355. New York: Oxford Univ. Press, 1971.
(Reprint of the 1947 article, no. **2**.)

379. "What Policies Toward Southern Africa?" *Current*, Mar. 1971, 50-68.
(Excerpt from the 1971 article "Hazardous Courses in Southern Africa," no. **368**.)

1972

BOOKS

380. *Memoirs, 1950-1963*. Boston: Little, Brown, 1972. viii, 368p.
This is the second volume of Kennan's memoirs (no. **306**). Kennan describes his first years at the Institute for Advanced Study, his part in decisions surrounding the Korean War, his time as Ambassador in Moscow, his intentions in the Reith Lectures (no. **136**) and the controversy surrounding them, and his Ambassadorship in Yugoslavia. Appended is an essay "The Soviet Union and the Atlantic Pact," written in 1952, in which Kennan questions the militarization of U.S. policy.
(Reprinted nos. **406,523**.)

ARTICLES

381. "After the Cold War: American Foreign Policy in the 1970's." *Foreign Affairs* 51 (Oct. 1972): 210-227.
Reviews U.S. policy problems in the East and West, and calls for putting aside the "rigidities of the Cold War." The U.S. should continue to support NATO, but it is not the best instrument to deal with many problems. The U.S. never acknowledged that NATO signalled giving up on peaceful unification of the continent. U.S. foreign aid programs in other areas have been misguided. The U.S. should be willing to work jointly with the Soviets and the Chinese to find solutions to some common problems.

382. "America's Love-Hate Affair with China." *The Observer*, 20 Feb. 1972, 9.
Looks at past U.S.-Chinese relations and comments on the reversal in U.S. policy on admission of the People's Republic to the U.N. Nixon's trip to China is primarily public relations, and will not advance understanding between the two peoples.

383. "'X' Plus 25: Interview with George Kennan." *Foreign Policy* 7 (summer 1972): 521.
Comments on changes on the international scene and in the Soviet Union since the "X" article (no. **2**) was written, describes ways U.S. policy did not follow prescriptions for containment laid down there, and calls for a middle ground between either "intimacy" or war with the Soviet Union.
(The interview is part of a section on the "X" article and containment. Reprinted nos. **393,405a,414**.)

COMMENTARIES

384. "Foreword." In *The Road to Yalta: Soviet Foreign Relations, 1941-1945*, by Louis Fischer, xi-xv. New York: Harper & Row, 1972.

Kennan describes how he came to know Fischer, notes their differences in interpretation and personality, and expresses admiration for Fischer's scholarship. [Speech at memorial service for Louis Fischer, Princeton University, Jan. 23, 1970.]

385. "Introduction." In *For the President: Personal and Secret--Correspondence between Franklin D. Roosevelt and William C. Bullitt*, edited by Orville H. Bullitt, v-xvi. Boston: Houghton Mifflin, 1972.
Reviews Bullitt's diplomatic career and characterizes him as "brilliant" but "impulsive."

386. "Reinhold Niebuhr, 1892-1971." *Proceedings of the American Academy of Arts and Letters and the National Institute of Arts and Letters*, 2d ser., 22 (1972): 79-83.
A commemorative address in which Kennan remembers Niebuhr's qualities as a teacher and philosopher.

387. "Research in Contemporary Events for the Writing of History." *Proceedings of the American Academy of Arts and Letters and the National Institute of Arts and Letters*, 2d ser., 22 (1972): 50-67.
Kennan introduces the two speakers, Arthur Schlesinger, Jr. and Barbara Tuchman, and talks about the meaning and pleasure of historical research.

TRANSLATIONS

387a. *Demokratia Ja Ylioppilasvasemmisto*. Translated by Aarne Valpola. Porvoo: Werner Söderström, 1972. 190, 18p.
(Not seen. Tr. of the 1968 work *Democracy and the Student Left*, no. **326**.)

388. *Diplomat in Prag, 1938-1940: Berichte, Briefe, Aufzeichnungen*. Translated by Hans Jürgen Baron von Koskull. Frankfurt: Goverts Krüger Stahlbers, 1972. 250p.
(Not seen. Tr. of the 1968 work *From Prague After Munich*, no. **329**.)

REPRINTS

388a. "American Diplomacy." In *Nationalist, Realist, and Radical: Three Views of American Diplomacy*, by Jerald A. Combs, 232-246. New York: Harper & Row, c1972.
(Excerpt from the 1951 work, no. **22**.)

389. "Let Peace Not Die of Neglect." In *The Korean War*, edited with an introduction by Lloyd C. Gardner, 148-157. New York: Quadrangle Books, 1972.
(Reprint of the 1951 article, no. **27**.)

390. *The Marquis de Custine and His "Russia In 1839."* London: Hutchinson, 1972. xii, 145p.
(Not seen. Another ed. of the 1971 work, no. **365**.)

390a. "Memoirs." In *Nationalist, Realist, and Radical: Three Views of American Diplomacy*, by Jerald A. Combs, 447-464. New York: Harper & Row, 1972.
(Excerpt from the 1967 work, no. **306**.)

391. "The Sources of Soviet Conduct." In *Recent American Foreign Policy: Conflicting*

Interpretations, rev. ed., edited by Lawrence S. Kaplan, 55-58. Homewood, Ill.: Dorsey Press, 1972. (Dorsey Series in American History.)
(Abridgement of the 1947 article, no. **2**.)

392. "The Sources of Soviet Conduct." In *The Cold War: A Study in U.S. Foreign Policy*, by Walter Lippmann, 53-75. New York: Harper, 1972.
(Reprint of the 1947 article, no. **2**. The first edition of this book by Lippmann criticizing the "X" article, published in 1947, did not contain this reprint.)

393. "What Future for U.S.-Soviet Policies?" *Current*, July 1972, 60-64.
(Reprint of the 1972 article "'X' Plus 25: Interview with George Kennan, no. **383**.)

1973

ARTICLES

394. "Detente: Diplomatic Opportunity . . . ." *Washington Post*, 8 Oct. 1973, sec.A, 16.
Outlines possibilities for détente, in controls on nuclear proliferation, and reducing tensions in Europe and in the Mid-East. Moscow's readiness for compromise is accompanied by more controls on ideological dissidents, but interference in these internal policies will not have the desired effect and will tie the hands of the U.S. negotiators. The best weapon for influencing these internal controls is the example of U.S. tolerance for diverse opinions.

395. "What We've Lost in Vietnam." *Washington Post*, 14 Jan. 1973, sec. B, 1.
Kennan briefly rebuts the arguments of the Administration for the efficacy of renewed bombing in Vietnam and recalls his testimony before the Senate Foreign Relations Committee in 1966 advising the "liquidation of unsound positions." He points out, also, that the bombings don't have public support.

396. "Soviet Dissidents." *Internasjonal Politikk* (Bergen) 4 (Oct./Dec. 1973): 839-845.
Describes the great gap in understanding between the Soviet dissidents and the leadership, points out the dilemmas for U.S. foreign policy in answering the demands of the dissidents, and voices doubts about the efficacy of this approach.

BOOK REVIEWS

397. "Noble Man," review of *Helmuth von Moltke: A Leader Against Hitler*, by Michael Balfour and Julian Frisby. *New York Review of Books*, 22 Mar. 1973, 3-6.
A sympathetic portrait of von Moltke, who was a friend of Kennan's. Kennan describes him as an atypical Nazi resister who was concerned with what path reconstruction would take after the war and wanted accommodation with the socialists--a thinker rather than as a man of action.

COMMENTARIES

398. "And Thank You Very Much." *New York Times*, 2 Dec. 1973, sec. 4, 17.
U.S. dependency on Arab oil is a short-sighted policy, hampering independence. The U.S. should use the occasion of the embargo to rectify the situation.

399. "Double Standards Over Mozambique." Letter to the editor. *The Times* (London),

25 July 1973, 17.

Chastises the liberals' "double standard" in denouncing as an atrocity the attack by Portuguese forces on civilians while ignoring similar attacks by blacks.

400. "Hamilton Fish Armstrong, 1893-1973." *Foreign Affairs* 51 (July 1973): 654-655.

An appreciation of the man who was editor of *Foreign Affairs* for many years.

401. "U.S.-Soviet Trade Trade: 'Favored' Is No Favor." Letter to the editor. *New York Times*, 25 Sept. 1973, 42.

"Most-favored-nation" trading status simply establishes normal trade relations with other countries, and there is no reason why the Soviet Union should not be among them.

TRANSLATIONS

401a. *Joji F. Kenam Kaikoroku Taiso Gaiko Ni Ikite Ge*. Translated by Okuhata Minoru. Tokyo: Yomiuri shimbumsha, 1973. 362p.

(Not seen. Tr. of the 1972 work *Memoirs, 1950-1963*, no. **380**.)

401b. *Joji F. Kenam Kaikoroku Taiso Gaiko Ni Ikite Jo*. Translated by Shimizu Toshio. Tokyo: Yomiuri shimbumsha, 1973. 476p.

(Not seen. Tr. of the 1967 work *Memoirs, 1925-1950*, no. **306**.)

401c. *Memoiren: 1950-1963*. Translated by Hans Jürgen von Koskull. Frankfurt: Goverts-Krüger-Stahlberg, 1973. 367p.

(Not seen. Tr. of the 1972 work *Memoirs, 1950-1963*, no. **380**.)

REPRINTS

402. "The Confusion of Ends and Means." In *The Soviet Crucible*, 4th ed., edited by Samuel Hendel, 261-263. North Scituate, Mass.: Duxbury Press, 1973.

(Reprint of the 1963 excerpt, no. **238**. See also no. **235**.)

403. "Demilitarizing the Cold War." In *Containment and the Cold War: American Foreign Policy Since 1945*, edited by Thomas G. Paterson, 117-130. Reading, Mass.: Addison-Wesley, 1973.

(Reprint of the 1958 reprint "A Chance to Withdraw Our Troops in Europe," no. **159**. See also nos. **123-124**.)

404. "Facing Reality: Disengagement Defended." In *Containment and the Cold War: American Foreign Policy Since 1945*, edited by Thomas G. Paterson, 142-156. Reading, Mass.: Addison-Wesley, 1973.

(Reprint of the 1959 article "Disengagement Revisited," no. **166**.)

405. "Firm Containment and Unalterable Counter-Force." In *Containment and the Cold War: American Foreign Policy Since 1945*, edited by Thomas G. Paterson, 18-33. Reading, Mass.: Addison-Wesley, 1973.

(Reprint of the 1947 article "The Sources of Soviet Conduct," no. **2**.)

405a. "Interview with George F. Kennan." In *Beyond Containment: U.S. Foreign Policy in Transition*, edited by Robert W. Tucker and William Watts, 3-16. Washington, D.C.:

Potomac Associates, 1973.
(Reprint of the 1972 article, "'X' Plus 25: Interview With George Kennan," no. **383**.)

406. *Memoirs, 1950-1963*. London: Hutchinson, 1973. x, 368p.
(Not seen. Another ed. of the 1972 work, no. **380**.)

407. "Vietnam and Containment." In *Containment and the Cold War: American Foreign Policy Since 1945*, edited by Thomas G. Paterson, 171-180. Reading, Mass.: Addison-Wesley, 1973.
(Reprint of the 1966 document "Statement of Hon. George Kennan, no. **289**.)

1974

ARTICLES

408. "Cold-Warrior Eyes Age of Detente: George Kennan Speaks Out, Maps New Career at 70," interview by Steve Neal. *Philadelphia Inquirer*, 21 Apr. 1974, sec.1, 3.
Part interview and part biographical description, this article quotes Kennan on Watergate, Kissinger, student rebellions, the Cold War and revisionist historians.

409. "Europe's Problems, Europe's Choices." *Foreign Policy* 14 (spring 1974): 3-16.
Disputes claims that a "Finlandization" of Western Europe is a necessary result if American troops are withdrawn, or of "Ostpolitik." Kennan reminds readers of his proposal for mutual withdrawal in 1957, and benefits he saw for that at the time.

410. "The Legacy of Woodrow Wilson." *Princeton Alumni Weekly*, 1 Oct. 1974, 11-13.
An appreciation of Wilson; Kennan confesses he is not in unqualified agreement with Wilson's political philosophy but praises his integrity of purpose, dedication, and effort to mold and articulate a place for the U.S. in international affairs.
[Address at Woodrow Wilson International Center for Scholars, Washington, D.C.]

411. "Streets Once Really Seen, or Seen in Dreams." *New Yorker*, 29 Apr. 1974, 41-61.
Recalling a visit to Leningrad in 1973 and describing every-day scenes there, provides an occasion to ruminate on urban vs. rural life, as well as pre-Revolutionary and Revolutionary Russia.

BOOK REVIEWS

412. "Between Earth and Hell," review of *Arkhipelag Gulag, 1918-1956*, pts. 1 and 2, by Alexander Solzhenitsyn. *New York Review of Books*, 21 Mar. 1974, 3-7.
Kennan predicts this work will have a major effect on the Soviet system, and cannot fail to have a humanizing influence.
(Reprinted no. **420**.)

REPRINTS

413. "The Ideology of Containment: The X Article." In *Caging the Bear: Containment and the Cold War*, edited by Charles Gati, 9-24. Indianapolis: Bobbs-Merrill, 1974.
(Reprint of the 1947 article "The Sources of Soviet Conduct," no. **2**)

414. "Mr. X Revisited: An Interview With George F. Kennan." In *Caging the Bear: Containment and the Cold War*, edited by Charles Gati, 27-39. Indianapolis: Bobbs Merrill, 1974.
(Reprint of the 1972 article "'X' Plus 25: Interview With George Kennan," no. **383**.)

415. *Russia, the Atom, and the West*. Westport, Conn.: Greenwood Press, 1974. ix, 116p.
(Not seen. Another ed. of the 1958 work, no. **136**.)

1975

DOCUMENTS

416. "Statement of George F. Kennan." In U.S. Congress. Senate. Committee on Foreign Relations. *Detente*. Hearings . . . 93d Cong. 2d sess. on United States Relations with Communist Countries. Aug. 15, 20-21, Sept. 10, 12, 18-19, 24-25, Oct. 1, 8, 1974, 60-89. Washington, D.C.: GPO, 1975.
Kennan sees nothing particularly new in "détente"--better relations with the Soviets have always been desirable. He warns against using trade relations to pressure the Soviets on emigration, and would like to see greater efforts in arms control.

BOOK REVIEWS

417. Review of *St. Petersburg and Moscow: Tsarist and Soviet Foreign Policy, 1814-1974*, by Barbara Jelavich. *Slavic Review* 34 (June 1975): 388-390.

COMMENTARIES

418. "Comment." *Survey*, winter/spring 1975, 29-36.
Kennan comments on leadership and strategy of Roosevelt, Churchill and Stalin, in response to papers from the symposium "Allied Leadership During World War II."

419. "The Meaning of Vietnam." *New York Review of Books*, 12 June 1979, 28.
In one of several contributions on the topic, Kennan urges resisting the impulse to intervene everywhere; not overreacting if "pseudocommunist" regimes are established in Third World countries; and beginning to exercise leadership in global conservation.
(Reprinted no. **421**.)

REPRINTS

420. "Between Earth and Hell." In *Aleksandr Solzhenitsyn: Critical Essays and Documentary Materials*, 2d ed., edited by John B. Dunlop, Richard Haugh, and Alexis Klimhoff, 501-511. New York: Collier Books, 1975.
(Reprint of the 1974 book review, no. **412**.)

421. "On Turning to Global Problems." *Current*, July 1975, 49.
(Reprint of the 1975 commentary "The Meaning of Vietnam," no. **419**.)

1976

ARTICLES

422. "Conversation With George Kennan." In *Conversations with Eric Sevareid: Interviews With Notable Americans*, 80-96. Washington, D.C.: Public Affairs Press, 1976.

In this interview conducted Sept. 7, 1975, Kennan discusses, among other topics, his intent in the "X" article (no. **2**), his disagreement with the militarization of U.S. policy and solidification of the division of Europe, the attraction of communism for young people, his own elitism, and the utility of summit meetings.

423. "From Containment to . . . Self-Containment: A Conversation with George F. Kennan," interview by George Urban. *Encounter*, Sept. 1976, 10-43.

A wide-ranging interview in which Kennan speaks his mind on a variety of topics. Characterizing himself as a mixture of conservative and liberal, he talks about his pessimism regarding the American political system, the evils of industrialization, requirements for self-government, his sympathy for a "meritocracy," problems inherent in the division of Europe, the West's preoccupation with the Soviet threat, and other issues.

(Reprinted nos. **448,463,634,638**.)

424. "Is Détente Worth Saving?" *Saturday Review*, 6 Mar. 1976, 12-17.

The idea of detente was oversold, and now there is a reaction to it. Although there are areas where no agreement with the Soviets is possible--Kennan reviews ideological differences and antagonisms before and after World War II--there are areas where collaboration is possible, and where the West could make a greater effort, particularly in nuclear proliferation.

["Adapted from remarks made at a meeting of Washington area Slavists, held under the auspices of the Kennan Institute."]

425. "Sind alle Russen 2,50 Meter gross? Der Westen übertreibt die Bedrohung von aussen und ist blind fur die Gefähren im Inneren." *Die Zeit*, 5 Mar. 1976, 3.

(See for annotation English translation 1976: "Are All Russians 8 Feet Tall. . . and Is the West Blind to the Threat from Within?" no. **429**.)

426. "The United States and the Soviet Union, 1917-1976." *Foreign Affairs* 54 (July 1976): 670-690.

A historical review of events and trends in relations between the U.S. and the U.S.S.R., from American reaction to the Russian Revolution to the stymied SALT talks. Although relations are at a low point in 1976, Kennan notes that a new generation of leaders in the U.S.S.R. should soon take over, while it is not impossible for U.S. policy to overcome some shortcomings of the past. He ends on a note of moderated optimism for improved relations.

DOCUMENTS

427. "Memorandum by the Counselor of the Department (Kennan) to the Secretary of State." In U.S. Dept. of State. *Foreign Relations of the United States, 1950.* Vol 2, *The United Nations; The Western Hemisphere*, 598-624. Washington, D.C.: GPO, 1976. (S1.1)

An analysis of the situation in Latin America after a fact-finding tour there. Kennan has little good to say about political and social conditions, warns against getting involved in internal politics, and rates the danger of communist influence in Latin America as more "psychological" than strategic.

COMMENTARIES

428. "George F. Kennan Replies." *Slavic Review* 35 (Mar. 1976): 32-36.
Kennan refutes some assertions concerning his support for militarization of the Cold War, made in a previous article by C. Ben Wright, and warns against the misuse of textual evidence.

TRANSLATIONS

429. "Are All Russians 8 Feet Tall . . . and Is the West Blind to the Threat from Within?" *Freedom at Issue*, Sept./Oct. 1976, 14-16.
Disputes the idea that "détente" in the 1970s was a sudden change in Soviet policy, constituting general agreement between East and West. By the same measure, recent actions are not a break with that policy. Not all the problems the West faces are Soviet-inspired, and the failure to face up to that reality does not serve the West well.
(Translation of the 1976 article "Sind alle Russen 2,50 Meter gross?" no. **425**. Reprinted nos. **430,438,455,634**.)

REPRINTS

430. "Are Russians Eight Feet Tall?" *Current*, Nov. 1976, 56-60.
(Reprint of the 1976 translation "Are All Russians 8 Feet Tall," no. **429**.)

1977

BOOKS

431. *The Cloud of Danger: Current Realities of American Foreign Policy*. Boston: Little, Brown, 1977. xiii, 234p.
An analysis of U.S. foreign policy problems. Kennan favors a regional approach, based on concrete realities. The U.S. is still too concerned with promoting abstract principles. An agenda is needed to relieve problems at home. Among the dangers are dependence on Arab oil and the arms race.
(Reprinted no. **445**. Excerpts reprinted nos. **439,446,634**.)

ARTICLES

432. "A Different Approach to the World: An Interview," interview with Martin Agronsky. *New York Review of Books*, 20 Jan. 1977, 12-17.
Touches on détente, policy in Southern Africa, the Mid-East, Iran, and China. Nuclear proliferation is out of control. The "X" article was a valid assessment of the situation at the time. The U.S. need not worry too much about an ideological challenge from the Soviets, but should concentrate on living up to its own standards of morality.

433. "Foreign Policy and the Professional Diplomat." *Wilson Quarterly* 1 (winter 1977): 148-157.

Emphasizes the influence of organized interest groups, rather than public opinion in deflecting U.S. policy from a rational course. The Foreign Service is hampered by a weakened State Department.
(Reprinted no. **447**.)

434. "A Plea by Mr. X 30 Years Later." *Washington Post* 11 Dec. 1977, sec. D, 1+.
Opposition to a balanced and realistic policy toward the Soviet Union now comes from the right, in contrast to the late 1940s, when the left's "naïve" view of the Soviets thwarted realistic policies. Militarization has taken over policy-making, and negotiation itself is being discredited, a stance the U.S. can ill afford.
[Address before the Council on Foreign Relations, Washington, D.C., Nov. 22, 1977.]
(Reprinted nos. **444,449,452,454,465**.)

DOCUMENTS

435. "International Control of Atomic Energy. [Extracts]. Memorandum by the Counselor (Kennan)." In U.S. Dept. of State. *Foreign Relations of the United States, 1950*. Vol 1. *National Security Affairs; Foreign Economic Policy*, 22-44. Washington, D.C.: GPO, 1977. (S1.1)

U.S. policy on nuclear weapons is ambiguous. It is unclear whether nuclear weapons are regarded as a necessity only because other nations have them or whether these are integral offensive/defensive alternatives. Before embarking on development of the hydrogen bomb, Kennan urges adopting a "no-first-use" policy and an effort to curb nuclear proliferation.

COMMENTARIES

436. "Some Thoughts on Stalin's Foreign Policy." *Slavic Review* 36 (Dec. 1977): 590-591.

Comments on the preceding article in the same issue by Robert Tucker on Stalin's foreign policy. Kennan agrees with Tucker in general but elaborates some specific points.

437. "Walter Lippmann, 1889-1974." *Proceedings of the American Academy of Arts and Letters and the National Institute of Arts and Letters*, 2d ser., 27 (1977): 54-58.

A commemorative tribute praising the style and substance of Lippmann's work.

REPRINTS

438. "Are All Russians 8 Feet Tall . . . and Is the West Blind to the Threat from Within?" *Military Review*, May 1977, 42-46.

(Reprint of the 1976 translation "Are All Russians 8 Feet Tall? no. **429**.)

439. "Let Panama Take the Consequences." *Wall Street Journal*, 16 Sept. 1977, 18.
(Excerpt from the 1977 work *The Cloud of Danger*, no. **431**. Kennan advocates giving up control over the Canal and reducing dependence on it.)

440. "The United States and the Soviet Union, 1917-1976." In *Two Hundred Years of American Foreign Policy*, edited by William P. Bundy, 142-180. New York: New York Univ. Press, 1977.

(Reprint of the 1976 article no. **426**.)

1978

ARTICLES

441. "Can Carter Handle Him? An Appeal for Thought," interview by Marilyn Berger. *New York Times Magazine*, 7 May 1978, 43+.

Kennan advocates a reassessment of U.S. policy toward the Soviets, to a more hopeful and less militaristic posture. He discusses reasons why he does not see the Soviets initiating a war, possibilities for negotiation, Soviet influence in Europe, American interventions abroad, and chances for Carter's "human rights" initiative. He says his views through the years have been "consistent."

COMMENTARIES

442. "George Kennan on Containment Reconsidered." *Foreign Affairs* 56 (Apr. 1978): 643-645.

In a letter to the editor, Kennan argues against Eduard Mark's contention that he contributed to a militarization of policy in 1947 and 1948. (See no. **695**.)

443. "A Last Warning: Reply to My Critics." *Encounter*, July 1978, 15-18.

Replies to attacks on his position on arms control and negotiation and the Soviet threat. Kennan says he has not abandoned containment, but that the situation has changed. Renewing the arms race is an act of "desperation."

(Reprinted nos. **466,638**.)

TRANSLATIONS

443a. *Wolken der Gefahr: Aktuelle Probleme der Amerikanischen Aussenpolitik*. Translated by Hartmut Velbinger. Munich: Tuduv-Verlagsgesellschaft, 1978. 244p.

(Not seen. Tr. of the 1977 work *The Cloud of Danger*, no. **431**.)

REPRINTS

444. "America's Relations with the Soviet Union." *Bulletin of the Atomic Scientists* 34 (June 1978): 21-23.

[Address before the Council on Foreign Relations, Washington, D.C., Nov. 1977.]
(Abridgement of the 1977 article "A Plea by Mr. X 30 Years Later," no. **434**. Reprinted no. **454**.)

445. *The Cloud of Danger: Some Current Problems of American Foreign Policy*. London: Hutchinson, 1978. 234p.

(Not seen. Another ed. of the 1977 work *The Cloud of Danger: Current Realities of American Foreign Policy*, no. **431**.)

446. "The Cloud of Danger." In *Decline of the West? George Kennan and His Critics*, 81-95. Washington, D.C.: Ethics and Public Policy Center, Georgetown Univ., 1978.

(Excerpt from the 1977 work, no. **431**.)

447. "Foreign Policy and the Professional Diplomat." In *Foreign Policy and the Democratic Process*, edited by Louis Halle and Kenneth Thompson, 14-26. Washington, D.C.: University Press of America, 1978.
(Reprint of the 1977 article, no. **433**. Article written for this 1978 collection.)

448. "From Containment . . . To Self-Containment." In *Decline of the West? George Kennan and His Critics*, 11-13. Washington, D.C.: Ethics and Public Policy Center, Georgetown Univ., 1978.
(Excerpt from the 1976 article, no. **423**.)

449. "Mr. X Reconsiders: A Current Assessment of Soviet American Relations." *Encounter*, Mar. 1978, 7-13.
[Address before the Council on Foreign Relations, Washington, D.C., Nov. 1977.]
(Reprint of the 1977 article "A Plea By Mr. X 30 Years Later," no. **434**. Reprinted no. **638**.)

450. "Moscow Embassy Telegram #511: 'The Long Telegram,' Feb. 22, 1946." In *Containment: Documents on American Policy and Strategy, 1945-1950*, edited by Thomas H. Etzold and John Lewis Gaddis, 50-63. New York: Columbia Univ. Press, 1978.
(Reprint of the 1969 document "The Chargé in the Soviet Union (Kennan) to the Secretary of State," no. **350**. See also no. **629**.)

451. "The Sources of Soviet Conduct." In *Containment: Documents on American Policy and Strategy, 1945-1950*, edited by Thomas H. Etzold and John Lewis Gaddis, 84-90. New York: Columbia Univ. Press, 1978.
(Excerpt from the 1947 article, no. **2**. See also no. **629**.)

452. "Soviet Doves and American Hawks." In *Decline of the West? George Kennan and His Critics*, 49-60. Washington, D.C.: Ethics and Public Policy Center, Georgetown Univ., 1978.
(Reprint of the 1977 article "A Plea By Mr. X 30 Years Later," no. **434**.)

453. *Soviet Foreign Policy, 1917-1941*. Westport, Conn.: Greenwood Press, 1978. 191p.
(Not seen. Another ed. of the 1969 work, no. **186**.)

454. "U.S.-Soviet Relations." *Current*, July/Aug. 1978, 36-41.
[Abridgement of address before the Council on Foreign Relations, Washington, D.C., Nov. 1977.]
(Reprint of the 1978 reprint "America's Relations With the Soviet Union, no. **444**. Original title: "A Plea By Mr. X 30 Years Later," no. **434**.)

455. "Western Decadence and Soviet Moderation." In *Decline of the West? George Kennan and His Critics*, 3-9. Washington, D.C.: Ethics and Public Policy Center, Georgetown Univ., 1978.
(Reprint of the 1976 translation "Are All Russians 8 Feet Tall?" no. **429**.)

1979

BOOKS

456. *The Decline of Bismarck's European Order: Franco-Russian Relations, 1875-1890*. Princeton, N.J.: Princeton Univ. Press, 1979. xii, 466p.

The first in a projected three-part study on the Franco-Russian Alliance and the coming of the First World War, this looks at the origins of the alliance, the breakdown of the Russo-German agreement, and the isolation of France. Kennan finds some characteristics of the age, which spurred it on to the final tragedy of 1914: extreme nationalism, acceptance of the inevitability of war, and a romantic conception of military conflict.

(See also *The Fateful Alliance*, no. **526**. Excerpt reprinted no. **468**.)

ARTICLES

457. "Ethics and Foreign Policy: An Approach to the Problem." In *Foreign Policy & Morality: Framework for a Moral Audit*, by Theodore M. Hesburgh and Louis J. Halle, 42-44. New York: Council on Religion and International Affairs, 1979.

One of five commentators on essays by Hesburgh and Halle, Kennan makes a distinction between governments and the individual. Governments, by their nature, encompass many beliefs and traditions, they do not have one moral purpose. Kennan comments that human rights are not absolute but exist as a part of complex rights and responsibilites in different polities.

458. "'Ich glaube nicht dass das zu offensiven Zwecken aufgestellt würde.' Ein Interview mit dem U.S.-Diplomaten und Historiker George F. Kennan über Nuklearwaffen, Enstparrung und Ost-West-Beziehungen," interview by Michael Herde. *Frankfürter Rundschau*, 28 Mar. 1979, 10.

(Not seen.)

459. "Morality, Politics, and Foreign Policy." In *Four Virginia Papers Presented at the Miller Center Forums, 1979*, edited by Kenneth W. Thompson, 3-29. Washington, D.C.: University Press of America, 1979.

Kennan returns to the theme of morality in foreign policy. The function of foreign relations--the advancement of the national interest--is not essentially a moral one, but moral principles affect its "style and quality." Morality is found in courtesy, generosity, avoidance of hardship to other nations, and avoidance of a major war. He touches on isolationism and obligations to Third World countries, foreign aid, Soviet expansionism, democracy, and the recognition of limitations. Followed by questions and answers.

460. "The President and His Ambassadors." In *Four Virginia Papers Presented at the Miller Center Forums, 1979*, edited by Kenneth W. Thompson, 95-106. Washington, D.C.: University Press of America, 1979.

In this discussion about whether the diplomat represents the President as a politician and leader of his party, or as the representative of the whole people, Kennan favors the latter role.

461. "Unione Sovietica e Distensione." *Relazioni Internazionali* (Milan) 43 (Aug. 25, 1979): 716-717.

The recent Soviet military buildup has drawn concern in the West, but neither the ideological nor the practical conditions for Soviet aggression seem to be present. The unleashing of a real war will depend on the militarization of East-West relations and other motivations.

DOCUMENTS

462. "The State of Strategic and Theater Deterrence." In U.S. Senate. Committee on Foreign Relations. *Perceptions: Relations Between the United States and the Soviet Union*, 335-339. Washington, D.C.: GPO, 1979. (Y4F76/2:P41)

This collection of essays by experts was intended to clarify issues as the SALT II talks approached. Kennan says the Soviets are unlikely to launch a major offensive outside their borders, though they might aid wars of liberation. Areas of potential conflict are Korea, the Near and Middle East, and Southern Africa. Any war will be affected by the degree of military competition between the two great powers; other values need to be given their place.

REPRINTS

463. "A Conversation: George F. Kennan and George Urban." In *Encounters with Kennan: The Great Debate*, 1-84. London: Frank Cass, 1979.

(Reprint of the 1976 article "From Containment to Self-Containment, a Conversation with George F. Kennan," no. **423**.)

464. "A Conversation: George F. Kennan and Melvin J. Lasky." In *Encounters with Kennan: The Great Debate*, 189-215. London: Frank Cass, 1979.

(Reprint of the 1960 article, "A Conversation With George Kennan," no. **187**.)

465. "Mr X Reconsiders." In *Encounters with Kennan: The Great Debate*, 111-122. London: Frank Cass, 1979.

(Reprint of the 1978 reprint, no. **449**. See no. **434** for original.)

466. "A Last Warning." In *Encounters with Kennan: The Great Debate*, 159-164. London: Frank Cass, 1979.

(Reprint of the 1978 commentary, no. **443**.)

467. *Soviet Foreign Policy, 1917-1941*. Huntington, N.Y.:
R.E. Kreiger, 1979. 192p.

(Not seen. Another ed. of the 1960 work, no. **186**.)

468. "Toward August 1914." *New Republic*, 3 Nov. 1979, 30-31.

(Excerpt from the 1979 work *The Decline of Bismarck's European Order*, no. **456**.)

1980

ARTICLES

469. "George F. Kennan on Washington's Reaction to the Afghan Crisis: 'Was This Really Mature Statesmanship?'" *New York Times*, 1 Feb. 1980, sec. A, 27.

The Soviet action in Afghanistan, abrupt and ill-considered, may signal the ascendance of hardliners in the Kremlin, but the American reaction forecloses diplomacy. The U.S. fixation on the military threat influences it to seek unstable allies and obscures the real problem in the Middle East, which is dependence on Arab oil.
(Reprinted: nos. **477-478**.)

470. "Die rote Armee in Kabul: Ende der Entspannung?" *Die Zeit*, 18 Jan. 1980, 5.
Kennan's contribution to this three-part article (with Richard Löwenthal and Dmitri Simes) is titled "Ein defensiver Schritt" ("A Defensive Move"). The Soviets are preoccupied with Afghan instability as a threat to them, but the internal dynamics of U.S. politics encourages an offensive interpretation of their military moves.

471. "Die russiche Gefahr ist viel Einbildung. Wider die Welle den Angstmacherei." *Die Zeit*, 11 Jan. 1980, 9.
Kennan argues against the current "alarmism" of Washington political opinion reacting to Soviet moves in Afghanistan. He blames both ideological blinders and cynical manipulation of facts and numbers for current pressure to build up NATO arms. Soviet security poses less threat to the West than Soviet weakness. Openly seeking destruction of the Soviet Union could unleash a terrible reaction. Success could open the way to unpleasant alternatives--including "Great-Russian chauvinists" long held in check.

472. "U.S.-Soviet Relations: Turning from Catastrophe." *Christianity and Crisis*, 26 May 1980, 155-158.
The U.S.-Soviet conflict has turned from an ideological to a military one. A war would never bring "victory," but the arms race continues. The U.S. needs leadership that will guide it toward nuclear weapons control and combat its propensity to dehumanize the enemy.
[Adapted from an address given in the Cathedral of St. John the Divine, New York, Mar. 23, 1980.]
(Reprinted no. **480**.)

473. "Warriors in the White House." *The Observer*, 10 Feb. 1980, 10.
The U.S. reaction to the Soviet occupation in Afghanistan is overly belligerent and deflects attention from the real problems in the Middle East--the Arab-Israeli conflict and dependence on Arab oil.

474. "Wir haben unsere Karten 'Überreizt', Amerikas Reaktion auf Afghanistan." *Der Spiegel*, 17 Feb. 1980, 146-149.
The Soviet invasion of Afghanistan points to the influence of a younger less experienced leadership, but the U.S. is overreacting with its unrealistic threat of massive retaliation. Faulty analysis of the situation results in errors of judgement in forming alliances in the Middle East.

DOCUMENTS

475. "Statement of Hon. George F. Kennan." In U.S. Conress. Senate. Committee on Foreign Relations. Subcommittee on Near Eastern and South Asian Affairs. *U.S. Security Issues and Policies in Southwest Asia*. Hearings . . 96th Cong., 2d sess. Feb. 6-7, 20, 27, Mar. 4, 18, 1980, 88-124. Washington, D.C.: GPO, 1980. (Y4F76/2:Se2/13)

Kennan's statement addresses avoiding a military conflict with the Soviets, the Iranian hostage crisis, U.S. dependence on Persian Gulf oil, the situation in Afghanistan, and what the American response should be to the Soviet invasion. Also included are "Excerpts from Interview of George Kennan, by Dan Rather on '60 Minutes,' Feb. 9, 1980," reprints of "George F. Kennan on Washington's Reaction to the Afghan Crisis," (no. **477**) and "The Sources of Soviet Conduct," (no. **2**).

(Excerpt reprinted no. **513**.)

TRANSLATIONS

476. *Tang ch'ien Mei'Kuo tui wai cheng ts'e ti hsien shih wei hsien ti yin yun.* Translated by Ch'ai Chin-ju and Liu Chueh-ch'ou. Beijing: Shang wu yin Kuan, 1980. 232p.

(Not seen. Tr. of the 1977 work *The Cloud of Danger*, no. **431**.)

REPRINTS

477. "George F. Kennan on Washington's Reaction to the Afghan Crisis." In U.S. Congress. Senate. Committee on Foreign Relations. Subcommittee on Near Eastern and South Asian Affairs. *U.S. Security Interests and Policies in Southwest Asia.* Hearings . . . 96th Cong. 2d sess. Feb. 6-7, 20, 27, Mar. 4, 18, 1980, 91-93. Washington, D.C.: GPO, 1980.

(Reprint of the 1980 article, no. **469**.)

478. "Imprudent Response to the Afghan Crisis?" *Bulletin of the Atomic Scientists* 38 (Apr. 1980): 7-9.

(Reprint of the 1980 article "George F. Kennan on Washington's Reaction to the Afghan Crisis," no. **469**.)

479. "The Sources of Soviet Conduct." In U.S. Congress. Senate. Committee on Foreign Relations. Subcommittee on Near Eastern and South Asian Affairs. *U.S. Security Interests and Policies in Southwest Asia.* Hearings . . . 96th Cong., 2d sess. Feb. 6-7, 20, 27, Mar. 4, 18, 1980, 95-104. Washington, D.C.: GPO, 1980.

(Reprint of the 1947 article, no. **2**.)

480. "U.S.-Soviet Relations: Turning from Catastrophe." *Current,* Sept. 1980, 50-55.

(Reprint of the 1980 article, no. **472**.)

1981

ARTICLES

481. "Beyond the Shadow of the Atom." *Boston Globe*, 29 Nov. 1981, sec. A, 15+.

Referring to *World Peace Through World Law*, by Grenville Clark and Louis B. Sohn, Kennan says the time may have come for a system of international law to deal with proliferation of nuclear weapons. The antinuclear movement is truly popular, backed by the inexorable logic of the uselessness of the nuclear weapon. Mutual cuts in weaponry can be made. A change in assessment of the Soviet Union is needed.

[Address on receiving Grenville Clark Prize, Hanover, N.H., Nov. 16.]

(Reprinted nos. **490,495,511-512,539.**)

482. "Cease This Madness." *Atlantic*, Jan. 1981, 25-28.
Reviews characteristics and historical experiences of Americans and Russians since the Bolshevik Revolution, which contribute not only to the East-West conflict but also to its total militarization. Kennan calls for overcoming "military fixations" and recognition of common purposes and problems.
[Adapted from address to 2d World Congress on Soviet and East European Studies, Garmisch, Germany, Oct. 1980.]
(Reprinted 1981 in a slightly different version, no. **493.**)

483. "Countdown zur Katastrophe--oder kann man Krieg vermeiden? Der ehemalige U.S.-Diplomat fördert die Abkehr vom 'militarisierten Nachdenken' über die sowjetisch-amerikanischen Beziehungen." *Frankfürter Rundschau*, 24 Oct. 1981, 14-15.
(Not seen.)

484. "Ein absurdes Overkill, Interview mit George F. Kennan zu seinem Abrüstungs-vorschlag (B.M.)." *Deutsche Volkszeitung* (Düsseldorf), 11 June 1981, 4.
(Not seen.)

485. "On the Nuclear Standoff and Its Insanity." *Los Angeles Times*, 24 May 1981, sec. 4, 1,3.
The arms race forges ahead, propelled by a momentum of its own. The nuclear weapon is useless, Kennan emphasizes, and the vicious cycle must be broken. Both the Americans and the Soviets have achieved multiple overkill. He proposes an immediate across-the-board reduction of nuclear weapons by 50%, followed by further cuts, and a joint Soviet-American Scientific Committee to study disposal and peaceful uses for nuclear power.
[From an address given May 19, 1981, upon receiving the Albert Einstein Peace Prize.]
(See for full text version the 1981 article "The Only Way Out of the Nuclear Nightmare Is By a Bold and Sweeping Gesture," no. **486**. Reprinted nos. **492,494,538.**)

486. "The Only Way Out of the Nuclear Nightmare Is By a Bold and Sweeping Gesture." *The Guardian*, 25 May 1981, 10.
[Address on receiving the Albert Einstein Peace Prize, May 19.]
(For annotation see the 1981 article "On the Nuclear Standoff and Its Insanity," a slightly abridged version, no. **485.**)

487. "Ost/Vest-forbindelsene. Sovjetregiment og den militaere trusel. (East-West Relations, the Soviet Regime and the Military Threat.") *Internasjonal Politikk* (Bergen) 4B (Suppl. 1981): 733-743.
(Not seen.)

488. "Reflections: Two Views of the Soviet Problem." *New Yorker*, 2 Nov. 1981, 55-56.
Kennan differentiates his views from those of his critics: he does not see the Soviet Union as implacably aggressive; rather, it is increasingly defensive and isolated. In this situation, the most important issue is arms control. Kennan calls for the "elimination of weapons of mass destruction."
(Reprinted no. **540.**)

489. "Die Supermächte auf Kollisionkurs. Verselbstständigen sich die Gruselbilder, die sie voneinander entwurfen?" *Die Zeit*, 28 Aug. 1981, 3.
(Not seen.)

TRANSLATIONS

489a. *Bismarcks europäisches System in der Auflösung: die franzözische-russische Annäherung 1875-1890*. Translated by Christa Armstrong. Frankfurt: Propylaen, 1981. 501p.
(Not seen. Tr. of the 1979 work *The Decline of Bismarck's European Order: Franco-Russian Relations, 1875-1890*, no. **456**.)

REPRINTS

490. "Beyond the Shadow of the Atom." *Congressional Record* 127 (Dec. 7, 1981): 29779-29800.
[Address on receiving the Grenville Clark Prize.]
(Reprint of the 1981 article, no. **481**.)

491. "A Modest Proposal." *New York Review of Books*, 16 July 1981, 14-16.
[Address on receiving the Albert Einstein Peace Prize.]
(Abridgement of the 1981 article "The Only Way Out of the Nuclear Nightmare is by a Bold and Sweeping Gesture," no. **486**. For annotation see no. **485**. See also nos. **492,494,538**.)

492. "The Nuclear Standoff: The Irrationality of Nuclear Weapons." *Current*, Sept. 1981, 3-7.
[Address on receiving the Albert Einstein Peace Prize.]
(Reprint of the 1981 article "On the Nuclear Standoff and Its Insanity," no. **485**. See also nos, **491,494,538**.

493. "Scholarship, Politics and the East-West Relationship." *Bulletin of the Atomic Scientists* 37 (May 1981): 4-7.
[Address at 2d World Congress on Soviet and East European Studies in Garmisch, Germany, Oct. 1980.]
(See for annotation the slightly different version in the 1981 article "Cease This Madness," no. **482**.)

494. "The Way Out of the Nuclear Dilemma." *Bulletin of Peace Proposals* 12 (Sept. 1981): 221-224.
[Address on receiving the Albert Einstein Peace Prize.]
(Reprint of the 1981 article "On the Nuclear Standoff and Its Insanity," no. **485**. See also nos. **491-492,538**.)

495. "World Peace Through Law--Two Decades Later." *Vital Speeches*, 15 Dec. 1981, 137-140.
[Address on receiving the Grenville Clark Prize.]
(Reprint of the 1981 article "Beyond the Shadow of the Atom," no. **481**. See also reprints 1982 and 1985: "On Nuclear War," nos. **511-512,539**.)

1982

BOOKS

495a. *The Nuclear Delusion*. New York: Pantheon, 1982. xxx, 208p.
(Not seen. See the expanded ed. no. **513** for annotation.)

ARTICLES

496. "America's Unstable Soviet Policy." *Atlantic*, Nov. 1982, 71-80.
Kennan reviews Soviet-American relations since World War II, recommends ways to defuse the dangerous situation in Central and Eastern Europe, including neutralization of Germany, and concludes that, unfortunately, internal U.S. politics plays more of a role in determining foreign policy than external events.
(Reprinted 1983 as "America and the Soviets," no. **521**.)

497. "Begegnungen mit Deutschland: Erinnerungen und Erfahrungen des Friedenspreisträgers." *Börsenblatt für Deutschen Buchhandel* (Frankfurt/Main) 38 (1982): 1367-1369.
(Not seen.)

498. "A Christian's View of the Arms Race." *Theology Today* 34 (summer 1982): 162-170.
The nuclear weapon is different from any other: its use would destroy civilization. Mankind must act as custodians, not destroyers, of the planet. Kennan proposes a "no-first-use" policy, better communication with Soviet adversaries, and ceasing to act as though war were the inevitable outcome of differences.
[Address at Princeton Theological Seminary, Apr. 27, 1982.]

499. "Ich möchte lieber mit unseren Regierungen einig sein, aber ich muss genau das Gegenteil vertreten. Rede von George F. Kennan anlässlich der Verleihung des Friedenspreise des Deutschen Buchhandels." *Deutsche Volkszeitung*, 14 Oct. 1982, 14.
(Not seen.)

500. "Nuclear Weapons and the Atlantic Alliance." With McGeorge Bundy, Robert S. MacNamara, and Gerard Smith. *Foreign Affairs* 60 (spring 1982): 753-768.
The authors call for U.S. acceptance of "no first use" and non-proliferation of nuclear weapons, and greater reliance on conventional forces in Europe.
(Reprinted no. **538a**.)

501. "Toward Peace on Two Fronts." *Christianity and Crisis*, 13 Dec. 1982, 398-402.
Obstacles to peace lie in the weapons race and the hostility of Soviet-American relations. The former is the more intractable problem. The U.S. seems committed to the arms race; it needs to find a way to control the military-industrial complex, for instance, cuts in weaponry, a "freeze," and agreement on "no first use", to reduce the danger. The U.S. also needs to recognize that it can disagree without resorting to war.
[Adapted from an address delivered at Union Theological Seminary, New York, Oct. 25, 1982.]

502. "The View from Russia." In *Witnesses to the Origins of the Cold War*, edited by Thomas T. Hammond, 27-33. Seattle: Univ. of Washington Press, 1982.
Refutes revisionist arguments for U.S. responsibility for the Cold War.

503. "Views from Another East Berlin." With Whitfield Bell, Jr. *Proceedings of the American Philosophical Society* 126 (1982): 472-480.
Briefly describes the countryside, history and social characteristics of the village of East Berlin, Penn., (where Kennan's farm is located), as an introduction to a history of the Berlin Improvement Society by Whitfield Bell, Jr.

504. [Omitted]

505. "Warum denn nicht Frieden? Die Rede des Friedenspreisträgers des Deutschen Buchhandels in der Frankfürter Paulskirche." *Frankfürter Allgemeine Zeitung*, 11 Oct. 1982, 9.
(Not seen.)

506. "Warum denn nicht Frieden? Den Krieg ernst und realistisch als Möglichkeit ausschliessen/Die Rede in der Paulskirche." *Süddeutsche Zeitung*, 11 Oct. 1982, 25.
(Not seen.)

COMMENTARIES

507. "A Major Voice in Debate Over Nuclear Arms." *U.S. News & World Report*, 26 Apr. 1982, 17-18.
In this interview, Kennan discusses his recent proposal for "no-first-use" policy of nuclear weapons and assesses the climate for arms reduction.
(Reprinted no. **510**.)

TRANSLATIONS

508. *Memoiren eines Diplomaten*. 2d ed. Translated by Heidi von Alten. Munich: Deutscher Taschenbuch-Verlag, 1982. 585p.
(Not seen. Tr. of *Memoirs, 1925-1950*, no. **306**.)

509. *Russland der Westen und die Atomwaffe*. With an essay by Marion Gräfin Dönhoff. Frankfurt: Ullstein, 1982. 126p.
(Not seen. Tr. of *Russia, the Atom, and the West*, no. **136**.)

REPRINTS

510. "Debate Over Nuclear Arms." *Current*, Oct. 1982, 39-43.
(Reprint of the 1982 commentary "A Major Voice in Debate Over Nuclear Arms," no. **507**.)

511. "On Nuclear War." *New York Review of Books*, 21 Jan. 1982, 8-12.
[Address on receiving the Grenville Clark Prize.]
(Reprint, slightly expanded, of the 1981 article, "Beyond the Shadow of the Atom," no. **481**. Reprinted nos. **512,539**. See also "World Peace Through Law," no. **495**.)

512. "On Nuclear War." *Current*, Feb. 1982, 26-32.
[Address on receiving the Grenville Clark Prize.]
(Reprint, slightly expanded, of the 1981 article "Beyond the Shadow of the Atom," no. **481**. Reprinted nos. **511,539**. See also "World Peace Through Law," no. **495**.)

1983

BOOKS

513. *The Nuclear Delusion: Soviet-American Relations in the Atomic Age*. Expanded ed. New York: Pantheon, 1983. xxx, 264p.

A collection of speeches, articles, and excerpts from interviews primarily from the 1970s and 1980s, in which Kennan addresses U.S. policy toward the Soviet Union and the nuclear arms race. In the introduction, Kennan explains his disagreements with official containment policy.
(See, for 1st ed., no. **495a**.)

ARTICLES

514. "Breaking the Spell." *New Yorker*, 3 Oct. 1983, 44-53.

Relations between the U.S. and U.S.S.R. are at a dangerously low point. The image of the Soviets in the U.S.--that they are insatiable in their quest for power and territory--is erroneous. There are possibilities for negotiation: arms control is the single most important issue; collaboration in cultural and scientific studies could be restored.
(Reprinted no. **524**.)

515. ["Remarks."] In *Fifty Years of Diplomatic Relations Between the United States and the Union of Soviet Socialist Republics*, 2-10. Washington, D.C.: Kennan Institute for Advanced Russian Studies, Woodrow Wilson International Center for Scholars, 1983. (Kennan Institute for Advanced Russian Studies Occasional Paper no.189.)

Kennan recalls his role in establishing diplomatic relations between the U.S. and U.S.S.R., and touches briefly on reasons for the Cold War, the arms race, and his hope for better rapport between the two nations. Also included is a talk by Anatoly Dobrynin and partial transcript of discussion.
(Excerpt reprinted no. **531**.)

516. "Zero Options." *New York Review of Books*, 12 May 1983, 3.

Deploring Reagan's decision to station intermediate-range nuclear weapons in Europe, Kennan proposes removal of all intermediate-range and tactical nuclear weapons by NATO and Warsaw Pact countries in Western Europe, and strengthening NATO's conventional forces. He repeats his support for a "no-first-use" policy.

DOCUMENTS

517. U.S. Dept. of State. Policy Planning Staff. *The State Department Policy Planning Staff Papers*. Foreword by George F. Kennan. Introduction by Anna Kasten Nelson. New York: Garland, 1983. 3v.

These are seminal position papers by the Policy Planning Staff, from 1947 to 1949, when Kennan was its director. Among the topics covered are European recovery and the Marshall Plan, trade with the Soviet Union and Eastern Europe, and policies in Greece, Italy the Mid-East, China, and Japan. Some, but not all, of these papers are also found in the State Department's *Foreign Relations of the United States* series. The introduction by Anna Kasten Nelson gives the background for the formation of the PPS and the significance of individual papers. In the Foreword, Kennan says these papers taken together indicate his philosophy of foreign policy.

TRANSLATIONS

518. *Atom-bedraget: forholdet mellom Sovietunionen og U.S.A i atomalderen.* Translated by Egil Johan Ree. Oslo: Gyldendal, 1983. 254p.
(Not seen. Tr. of *The Nuclear Delusion*, no. **513**.)

519. *Im Schatten der Atombombe: e. Analyse d. ameriken-sowjet Beziehungen von 1974 bis heute*. Translated by Hainer Kober. Cologne: Kiepenheuer und Witsch, 1983. 299p.
(Not seen. Tr. of *The Nuclear Delusion*, no. **513**.)

520. *Memoiren eines Diplomaten.* 4. ed. Translated by Heide von Alten. Munich: Deutscher Taschenbuch-Verlag, 1983. 595p.
(Not seen. Tr. of *Memoirs, 1925-1950*, no. **306**.)

REPRINTS

521. "America and the Soviets: America's Unstable Policy," *Current*, Feb. 1983, 43-57.
(Reprint of the 1982 article "America's Unstable Soviet Policy," no. **496**.)

522. *Memoirs, 1925-1950.* New York: Pantheon Books, 1983. 583p.
(Another ed. of the 1967 work, no. **306**.)

523. *Memoirs, 1950-1963.* New York: Pantheon Books, 1983. viii, 372p.
Contains a new Postscript.
(Another ed. of the 1972 work, no. **380**.)

524. *Soviet-American Relations: Breaking the Spell.* Boston: Council for a Livable World Education Fund, 1983. 12p.
(Reprint of the 1983 article "Breaking the Spell," no. **514**.)

1984

BOOKS

525. *American Diplomacy.* Expanded ed. Chicago: Univ. of Chicago Press, 1984. xii, 179p.
The full text of the 1951 work *American Diplomacy, 1900-1950*, no. **22**, with a new Foreword and two lectures given at Grinnell College in 1984, in which Kennan comments on the effects of popular opinion in the Korean and Vietnam wars and on the influence of the militarization of the Cold War on American society.

526. *The Fateful Alliance: France, Russia and the Coming of the First World War*. New York: Pantheon, 1984. xx, 300p.

The second in a projected three-part study of the forging of the Franco-Russian Alliance and the coming of the First World War, this details the diplomatic negotiations, 1890-1894, and the personalities and compulsions behind them. Kennan is critical of the purely military nature of the agreement; what political motivations there were behind the Alliance were backward-looking, a "delayed response" to events of the 1870s and 1880s.

(See also *The Decline of Bismarck's European Order*, no. **456**.)

527. ______. Manchester (Eng.): Manchester Univ. Press, 1984. xx, 300p.

(Not seen.)

ARTICLES

528. "Reflections: Two Letters." *New Yorker*, 24 Sept. 1984, 55-80.

Kennan looks at attitudes and issues separating the Americans and the Soviets at a time when relations are at a particularly low point. To the American, the Russians' obsessive secrecy, internal security, and distortion of history are barriers to understanding. From the Russian viewpoint, what is hard to comprehend is the Americans' lack of desire for negotiation, failure to ratify the SALT agreement, and failure to renounce first use of nuclear weapons.

COMMENTARIES

528a. "World War I; Then, II; Then . . . ." *New York Times*, 11 Nov., 1984, sec.E, 21.

In this Veterans Day essay, Kennan reminds readers of the awful devastation of the two world wars, which should give pause to any nation's rationale for an aggression based on the illusion that it is "more virtuous, deserving and generally glorious than the others."

TRANSLATIONS

529. *A alucinaçâo nuclear*. Translated by Christina Correia. Mem Martins: Europa-America, 1984. 247p.

(Not seen. Tr. of *The Nuclear Delusion*, no. **513**.)

530. *Le mirage nucléaire: les relations américano-soviétiques à l'âge de l'atome*. Translated by Antoine Berman. Paris: La Découverte, 1984. 261p.

(Not seen. Tr. of *The Nuclear Delusion*, no. **513**.)

REPRINTS

531. "A Plea for Diplomacy." *Harper's*, Apr. 1984, 9-11.

(Excerpt from the 1983 article ["Remarks"], no. **515**.

532. *Soviet-American Relations, 1917-1920*. Vol. 1, *Russia Leaves the War*. New York: Norton, 1984. xiii, 544p.

(Not seen. Another ed. of the 1956 work, no. **97**.)

533. ______. Vol. 2, *The Decision to Intervene*. New York: Norton, 1984. xii, 513p.

(Not seen. Another ed. of the 1958 work, no. **138**.)

533a. *The Nuclear Delusion*. London: Hamilton, 1984. 320p.
(Not seen. Another ed. of the 1983 work, no. **513**.)

1985

ARTICLES

534. "Flashbacks." *New Yorker*, 25 Feb. 1985, 52-69.
A personal reminiscence of Kennan's time in the Soviet Union, from the early days of establishing relations to the Stalinist era.

535. "The President's Choice: Star Wars or Arms Control." With Robert McNamara, Gerard Smith, and McGeorge Bundy. *Foreign Affairs* 63 (winter, 1984/1985): 264-278.
An appeal to President Reagan to set aside the "Star Wars" missile deterrent project in favor of negotiation with the Soviet Union. "Star Wars" will not make nuclear weapons obsolete, nor will it restrain the arms race; it will threaten the ABM treaty in place.

COMMENTARIES

536. "By the Light of the Midnight Sun." *House and Garden*, Apr. 1985, 178-179+.
Describes the pleasures and routines at the Kennans' summer home on the southeastern coast of Norway.

TRANSLATIONS

537. *O Declínio da Ordem Européia de Bismarck*. Translated by Fernando de Azevedo Correa, edited by Dinorah O. Mendes. Brasília: Editóra Universidade de Brasília, 1985. 486p.
(Not seen. Tr. of the 1979 work *The Decline of Bismarck's European Order*, no. **456**.)

REPRINTS

538. "Like Lemmings Heading for the Sea." In *George Kennan on NATO, Nuclear War, and the Soviet Threat*, edited with an introductory essay by Phil Braithwaite, 23-32. Evesham (Eng.): West Midlands CND Sales, 1985.
[Address on accepting the Albert Einstein Peace Prize.]
(Reprint of the 1981 article "On the Nuclear Standoff and its Insanity," no. **485**.)

538a. "Nuclear Weapons and the Atlantic Alliance." In *The Nuclear Controversy, a Foreign Affairs Reader*, edited and with an introduction by William P. Bundy, 23-40. New York: New American Library, 1985.
(Reprint of the 1982 article no. **500**.)

539. "On Nuclear War." In *George Kennan on NATO, Nuclear War, and the Soviet Threat*, edited with an introductory essay by Phil Braithwaite, 33-39. Evesham (Eng.): West Midlands CND Sales, 1985.
[Address on receiving the Grenville Clark Prize.]

(Reprint of the 1981 reprint "World Peace Through Law," no. **511**. See also nos. **481,495**.)

540. "Reflections: Two Views on the Soviet Problem." In *George Kennan on NATO, Nuclear War, and the Soviet Threat*, edited with an introductory essay by Phil Braithwaite, 40-48. Evesham (Eng.): West Midlands CND Sales, 1985.
(Abridgement of the 1981 article, no. **488**.)

541. *Soviet Foreign Policy, 1917-1941*. Malabar, Fla.: R.E. Kreiger, 1985. 191p.
(Not seen. Another ed. of the 1960 work, no. **186**.)

1986

ARTICLES

542. "Back From the Brink." With McGeorge Bundy, Morton H. Halperin, William W. Kaufmann, Robert S. McNamara, Madeline O'Donnell, Leon V. Sigal, Gerard C. Smith, Richard H. Ullman, and Paul C. Warnke. *Atlantic*, Aug. 1986, 35-41.
Joined by other scholars and leaders in the field, the original authors of "Nuclear Weapons and the Atlantic Alliance" (no. **500**) again make a forceful case for a "no-first-use" nuclear weapons policy and warn that nuclear weapons in NATO's front-line defenses could do more to trigger a crisis than act as a deterrent.

543. "The Curious Monsieur Cyon." *American Scholar* 55 (autumn 1986): 449-475.
A biographical portrait of a noted Russian physiologist in the 1860s, who became a controversial figure in his adherence to conservative anti-positivism. He was later an émigré in France and Switzerland, and played a part in promoting the Franco-Russian alliance. Kennan sees his life reflecting an important epoch in European history. (Cyon also figures briefly in Kennan's *The Decline of Bismarck's European Order*, no. **456**.)

544. "History, Literature and the Road to Peterhof." *New York Times Book Review*, 29 Jun. 1986, 1, 42.
Kennan returns to the theme of his article "It's History, But Is It Literature?" (no. **169**) and expands upon it. He discusses historical "objectivity" and the way both literary and historical writers seek to illuminate truth and the human condition. [Adapted from an address at the American Academy of Arts and Letters, May 21, 1986.]

545. "Morality and Foreign Policy." *Foreign Affairs* 64 (winter 1985/86): 205-218.
Returning to the theme expressed in *American Diplomacy, 1900-1950* (no. **22**), Kennan clarifies his position. The universalistic moral principles appealed to in the past by American statesmen are ambiguous as guides to action and they have not been uniformly applied. Morality in foreign policy would be better defined as a recognition of the national interest, realization of one's own limitations, and honesty and openness of purpose.
(Reprinted nos. **551,584a**.)

546. "Die Theatrik des Moralismus vermeiden--ein Plädoyer gegen die Träume von Welthegemonie." *Die Zeit*, 21 Feb. 1986, 39-42.
(Not seen.)

PAMPHLETS

547. *George F. Kennan on Russian Diplomacy in the 19th Century and the Origins of World War I.* Washington, D.C.: Kennan Institute for Advanced Russian Studies, Woodrow Wilson International Center for Scholars, 1986. 16p. (Special Report. Kennan Institute for Advanced Russian Studies.)

A transcript of Kennan's remarks discussing his research of the Franco-Russian Alliance of 1894 and events leading to World War I, followed by summaries of his replies to questions, which relate misconceptions and mistakes of the 19th Century to present-day issues. His works, *The Decline of Bismarck's European Order* (no. **456**) and *The Fateful Alliance* (no. **521**), are the first two volumes of a projected three part study clarifying the failures of understanding which brought about this catastrophic event.

[Remarks at the Kennan Institute for Advanced Russian Studies, Apr. 2, 1985.]

BOOK REVIEWS

548. "In the American Mirror," review of *Cycles of American History*, by Arthur Schlesinger, Jr. *New York Review of Books*, 6 Nov. 1986, 3-6.

Kennan discusses realism and morality in American foreign policy, the place of human rights in foregn policy, and whether structural changes, particularly Constitutional amendments, are needed to conduct foreign relations successfully in the future.

549. "A New Philosophy of Defense," review of *Making Europe Unconquerable: The Potential of a Civilian-Based Deterrence and Defense*, by Gene Sharp. *New York Review of Books*, 13 Feb. 1986, 3, 6.

Kennan sees much to praise about this proposal for defense strategy for non-nuclear countries. Avoiding the dangers of nuclear proliferation, and the bankruptcy of a nuclear defense, it requires reliance on and development of a civil defense, internal institutions, self-confidence, and self-discipline.

TRANSLATIONS

550. *Amerika Gaikô 50-nen.* Translated by Kondô Shin'ichi, Iida Tôji, and Aruga Tadashiyaku Zohoban. Tokyo: Iwanami Shoten, 1986. vi, 258p.

(Not seen. Tr. of the 1984 work *American Diplomacy*, expanded ed., no. **525**.)

REPRINTS

551. "Moral Restraints In Foreign Policy." *Current*, May 1986, 13-19.

(Abridgement of the 1986 article "Morality and Foreign Policy, no. **545**.)

1987

ARTICLES

552. "Containment Then and Now." *Foreign Affairs* 65 (spring 1987): 885-890.

Kennan details his argument that containment was never primarily a military doctrine. Furthermore, the situation now is much different: communism is not the political-ideological threat it was in the immediate postwar years. Threats today are the arms race and environmental destruction--it is these that need containment. (Part of an anniversary issue remembering the publication of the "X" article, no. **2**.)

553. "Eine Wasserscheide zwischen Angst und Hoffnung, kann der Marshall-Plan heute einen Weg in die Zukunft Europas weisen?" *Die Zeit*, 3 Jul. 1987, 52.
(Not seen.)

554. "Reflections on Containment." In *Containing the Soviet Union: a Critique of U.S. Policy*, edited by Terry L. Deibel and John Lewis Gaddis, 15-19. Washington, D.C.: Pergamon Brassey's International Defense Publishers, 1987.
"Containment", Kennan says, when he used the term in 1947, was directed primarily at the Soviet Union as a political threat; he did not think it was much of a military threat. Soviet military strength is now formidable; yet it still is not the greatest problem the U.S. faces. "Containment" could be better directed at the arms race and other global problems which threaten world political stability.

PAMPHLETS

555. *George F. Kennan on Russian Society and U.S.-Soviet Relations: A Special Report.* Washington, D.C.: Kennan Institute for Advanced Russian Studies, Woodrow Wilson International Center for Scholars, 1987. 18p.
In a brief talk given at the commemoration of the tenth anniversary of the Kennan Institute, Kennan outlines segments of Russian society--the common people, the nomenklatura, the intelligentsia, and the leadership--and proposes that a more hopeful course for U.S. policy is to find areas of agreement and collaboration, rather than to force changes the leadership could not survive.

COMMENTARIES

556. "Foreword." In *The Pathology of Power*, by Norman Cousins, 9-15. New York: Norton, 1987.
The nuclear weapon is different in kind from other weapons and will not resolve conflicts. The arms race itself is a threat to U.S. security, and it lacks the leadership to solve these problems. Cousins helps point the way to solutions.

557. "The Mission in Moscow." *Newsweek*, 13 July 1987, 7.
Security of the diplomatic mission in Moscow would be easier if its size were reduced. The U.S. cannot seem to decide whether its goal is to prepare for or avert war with the Soviet Union.

REPRINTS

558. "The Sources of Soviet Conduct." *Foreign Affairs* 65 (spring 1987): 852-868.
(Reprint of the 1947 article, no. **2**. Part of an anniversary issue with comments on the "X" article.)

1988

ARTICLES

559. "The Marshall Plan and the Future of Europe." *Transatlantic Perspectives*, winter 1988, 3-7.

Reviews the background and purposes of the Marshall Plan and its success. "Containment" was meant to provide economic and political stabilization, as a basis for negotiated settlement. Kennan outlines the rationale and possibilities for breaking down barriers in the East-West relationship.

560. "Obituary for the Cold War," interview by Nathan Gardels. *New Perspectives Quarterly*, summer 1988, 48-51.

Changes have come about in the Soviet Union, primarily as a result of internal pressures. If anything, U.S. over-militarization of its relations with the Soviets hindered the "mellowing" process. Gorbachev's *perestroika* is irreversible--there is no returning to the terror of the Stalin era. The Cold War is outmoded. (Reprinted no. **563a**.)

BOOK REVIEWS

561. "The Buried Past," review of *Memoirs*, by Andrei Gromyko. *New York Review of Books*, 27 Oct. 1988, 3+.

562. "The Gorbachev Prospect," review of *Perestroika*, by Mikhail Gorbachev. *New York Review of Books*, 21 Jan. 1988, 3+.

Calling Gorbachev's program for the U.S.S.R. "revolutionary," Kennan outlines the fragility of his position and the difficulties ahead. Ideological conflict will continue, but peacefully. For better relations with the Soviets, Americans must learn different attitudes from the "belligerant posturing" of the past.

COMMENTARIES

563. "The Gorbachev Prospect: An Exchange." With Josef Skvorecky. *New York Review of Books*, 17 Mar. 1988, 44.

Replies to Skvorecky's objections that Gorbachev is less an agent of change than Kennan put forth in "The Gorbachev Prospect," (no. **562**).

REPRINTS

563a. "Learning to Live without a Soviet Threat." *Harper's*, Nov. 1988, 17-19.

(Excerpt from the 1988 article "Obituary for the Cold War," no. **560**.)

1989

BOOKS

564. *Sketches from a Life*. New York: Pantheon Books, 1989. xiv, 365p.

A collection of journal entries, which are Kennan's personal observations and descriptions of places and people during his travels all over the world, from 1927 through 1988.

(Excerpt reprinted no. **572**.)

ARTICLES

565. "After the Cold War." *New York Times Magazine*, 5 Feb. 1989, 32-33+.
Credits Gorbachev with making bold and intelligent moves to end the Cold War. While we can expect relations between the U.S. and the U.S.S.R. to improve, we cannot expect them to be very close, since the two countries are so different. Kennan suggests normalization of trade, progress in arms control, and collaboration on environmental issues and space research.

565a. "George F. Kennan on the Crisis within the Soviet System," interview by Robert Travis Scott and Robert Guldin. *Arms Control Today*, Sept. 1989, 3-9.
Kennan predicts that after the recent revolutionary events in the Soviet Union domestic problems will overshadow those of foreign policy. The opportunity exists for mutual reduction of forces in Europe. The Strategic Arms Reduction Talks (START) are a beginning, but could go further. He discusses his views on negotiating positions, on the outlines of a reunified Europe, on the implications of Sino-Soviet normalization, and reiterates his position on "no first use" of nuclear weapons.

566. "The History of Arnold Toynbee." *New York Review of Books*, 1 June 1989, 19-22.
An appreciation of Toynbee as a historian. Kennan says that though he disagrees with Toynbee's quest for "uniformities" in world history, he should be remembered as a great scholar who undertook a "panoramic" study of history.
[Address accepting the Toynbee Prize, 1988-1989, at the Institute for Advanced Study, Princeton University.]

567. "Just Another Great Power." *New York Times*, 9 Apr. 1989, sec. 4, 25.
Introductory statement made by Kennan in testimony before the Senate Foreign Relations Committee on Apr. 4, 1989. (See no. **577** "Statement of Hon. George F. Kennan," for annotation.)

568. "This Is No Time for Talk of German Reunification." *Washington Post*, 12 Nov. 1989, sec. D, 1-2.
The lack of an overall European security framework--and the part that will be played by both the alliances with forces stationed in Germany--makes immediate unification inadvisable, from the standpoint of preserving stability. NATO needs to redefine its purpose.
(Reprinted nos. **571,573**.)

PAMPHLETS

569. *The German Problem: A Personal View*. Washington, D.C.: American Institute for Contemporary German Studies, Johns Hopkins Univ., 1989. 15p. (German issues, 6.)
In these remarks made before the fall of the Berlin Wall, Kennan views the strong Allied military presence in Germany as the greatest impediment to successful German unification and integration into Europe, while the movement toward European integration is a positive course. He reviews aspects of U.S. policy on Germany with which he was at odds over the years.

COMMENTARIES

570. "Introduction." In *Empire of the Czar: A Journey through Eternal Russia*, by the Marquis de Custine, foreword by Daniel J. Boorstin, xxi-xxxvi. New York: Doubleday, 1989.

An adaptation from Kennan's book on Custine (no. **365**), in which he gives a brief history of Custine, his reasons for visiting Russia, influences on him, and the reception of his book in Russia.

REPRINTS

571. "At Issue: Should Germans Be Allowed to Reunify, If They Want to Do So Soon?" *Editorial Research Reports* (Dec. 22, 1989): 725.

(Reprint of the article "This Is No Time for Talk of German Reunification," no. **568**.)

572. "The Last Wise Man." *Atlantic*, Apr. 1989, 39-47+.

(Excerpts from the 1989 work *Sketches from a Life*, no. **564**.)

573. "Reunification--Not Yet." *The Guardian*, 13 Nov. 1989, 23.

(Reprint of the article "This Is No Time for Talk of German Reunification," no. **568**.)

574. *Soviet-American Relations, 1917-1920*. Vol. 1, *Russia Leaves the War*. Princeton, N.J.: Princeton Univ. Press, 1989. xiii, 544p.

(Not seen. Another ed. of the 1956 work, no. **97**.)

575. *Soviet-American Relations, 1917-1920*. Vol. 2, *The Decision to Intervene*. Princeton, N.J.: Princeton Univ. Press, 1989. xii, 513p.

(Not seen. Another ed. of the 1958 work, no. **138**.)

1990

ARTICLES

576. "On the Soviet Union and Eastern Europe." *New York Review of Books*, 1 Mar. 1990, 7.

This is the introductory statement from hearings before the Senate Foreign Relations Committee, Jan. 17, 1990. (See no. **583**, "Statement of Hon. George F. Kennan" for annotation.)

DOCUMENTS

577. "Statement of Hon. George F. Kennan . . . ." In U.S. Congress. Senate. Committee on Foreign Relations. *The Future of U.S.-Soviet Relations*. Hearings . . . 101st Congress, 1st sess. Apr. 4, 12, 19, and May 3, 15, 18, and June 1 and 20, 1989, 3-36. Washington, D.C.: GPO, 1990.

Some tensions still remain after the radical changes in the Soviet Union, but it is no longer a military opponent and relations can assume a normality absent during the Cold War. Kennan thinks the U.S. has not been responsive in arms control initiatives. He urges some action in NATO and on the defense budget in

recognition of *perestroika* and *glasnost*. The "nationalities question" has the potential to pull the Soviet Union apart. Kennan favors gradual change, in Russia and in Eastern Europe.
(See also the 1989 article "Just Another Great Power," no. **567**.)

BOOK REVIEWS

578. "Witness," review of *The Uses of Adversity: Essays on the Fate of Central Europe*, by Timothy Garton Ash. *New York Review of Books*, 1 Mar. 1990, 3-6.
Kennan finds in the split between the public and private self, described by Ash, and the "pretense" of "outward conformity" to Communist life, shared by both the regime and people, a source of the spectacularly sudden collapse of the Communist regimes in the Soviet Union and Eastern Europe.

COMMENTARIES

578a. "Foreword." In *Before the Storm: Memories of My Youth in Old Russia*, by Marion, Countess Dönhoff, translated by Jean Steinberg, vii-x. New York: Knopf, 1990.
Kennan remarks that this memoir serves a valuable historical purpose in detailing a civilization and way of life which was obliterated by the war. (Marion Dönhoff later became an editor and publisher of *Die Zeit*.)

REPRINTS

579. "America and the Russian Future." *Foreign Affairs* 69 (spring 1990): 157-166.
(Abridgement of the 1951 article, no. **25**.)

1991

ARTICLES

580. "Communism in Russian History." *Foreign Affairs* 69 (winter 1990/91): 168-186.
A brief review of Russian political history from the rise of late-19th-Century revolutionary movements to Gorbachev. Kennan sees tragic elements in the failure of the Communists to distinguish between ends and means in their idealistic attempt to avoid the evils of capitalism. The political, economic, and imperial changes embarked upon by the reformers are more far-reaching than anything in Russia since the 18th Century, and will be an immense undertaking.
(Reprinted no. **585**.)

581. "Commentary." *Diplomatic History* 15 (fall 1991): 539-543.
An analysis of "The Novikov Telegram," an assessment of U.S. foreign policy by the Soviet Ambassador to the U.S., written in Sept. 1946. Kennan surmises that the document, which saw in postwar U.S. policy the aggressive pursuit of global dominance, was commissioned by Molotov to strengthen support for his own hard-line policies.

DOCUMENTS

582. *Measures Short of War: The George F. Kennan Lectures at the National War College, 1946-1947*, edited by Giles D. Harlow, and George C. Maerz. Washington,

D.C.: National Defense Univ. Press, 1991. xxxiii, 326p. (D5.402:M46)

A collection of thirteen lectures and one unpublished paper by Kennan, which brings together his analyses on some problems of the U.S. and the international scene at the time: policy toward the U.S.S.R, national security policy formulation, the state of the world and diplomacy in general.

583. "Statement of Hon. George F. Kennan . . . ." In U.S. Congress. Senate. Committee on Foreign Relations. Subcommittee on European Affairs. *The Future of Europe*. Hearings . . . 101st. Congress, 2d sess. Dec. 13, 1989, Jan 17, Feb. 1, 22, Mar. 1, 7, 21-22, 28-29, May 9, June 12, 1990, 74-93. Washington, D.C.: GPO, 1991.

Outlines the unstable situation in the Soviet Union and Eastern Europe, and recommends U.S. initiatives in removing trade barriers, reduction of conventional forces in Europe, and restructuring European security. New economic and political relationships in Europe should come from the Europeans themselves. Kennan favors gradual progress toward German reunification, and he points out the differences between the present situation in Eastern Europe and that in Europe at the time of the Marshall Plan.

(See also "On the Soviet Union and Eastern Europe," no. **576**.)

COMMENTARIES

584. "If the Kremlin Can't Rule." *Washington Post*, 3 Feb. 1991, sec. C, 1, 3.

It apppears likely that pressures for independence from the Baltic countries and the fifteen republics will prevail in breaking apart the U.S.S.R. Kennan commends the "restraint" of President Bush in influencing the situation.

REPRINTS

584a. "Morality and Foreign Policy." In *Morality and Foreign Policy: Realpolitik Revisited*, edited by Kenneth M. Jensen and Elizabeth P. Faulkner, 59-76. Washington, D. C.: United States Institute of Peace, 1991.

(Reprint of the 1986 article, no. **545**.)

585. "Communism in Russian History." *Current*, May 1991, 31-98.

(Abridgement of the 1991 article, no. **580**.)

1992

ARTICLES

585a. "Authors Talk To Voters," interview by Sarah Gold. *Publishers Weekly*, 17 Aug. 1992, 29.

Kennan sees a need for change in the U.S. political system if it is to improve its handling of foreign policy. He recommends a "Council of State" of private individuals divorced from politics to study and advise on foreign affairs.

586. "The Original Planning Staff." *Foreign Service Journal* 69 (Sept. 1992): 24-25.

Kennan reviews the purposes and organization of the State Dept.'s Policy Planning Staff when it was first constituted under his direction.

BOOK REVIEWS

587. "Keeping the Faith," review of *Summer Meditations*, by Vaclav Havel. *New York Review of Books*, 24 Sept. 1992, 3.

COMMENTARIES

588. "For Russian Troops, a House to Go Home to." *Washington Post*, 8 Nov. 1992, sec. C, 7.

Kennan suggests that the U.S. step in to relieve the housing shortage needed for returning Russian troops from the Baltics; he sees a precedent for this in the American Famine Relief effort in the 1920s and the Marshall Plan after World War II.

589. "The G.O.P. Won the Cold War? Ridiculous." *New York Times*, 28 Oct. 1992, 21.

The Cold War was costly to both sides, and the U.S. bears some responsibility for prolonging it. A single political party cannot claim credit for its dénouement. Now that the Cold War is over, serious problems are emerging, which call for a reexamination of the role of the U.S. and its policies, rather than complacent satisfaction.

REPRINTS

590. "The Unifying Factor." *World Policy Journal* 9 (fall/winter 1992): 795-800.

An excerpt in which Kennan envisions a U.S. that advances its goals peacefully in the wider world; becomes a cosmopolitan nation in trade, immigration and culture; and finds solutions to domestic problems through development that does not destroy the environment or break up communities. The "unifying factor" is that the domestic needs of the U.S. no longer have purely domestic solutions: today's domestic solutions must be sought in a global context.

(Excerpt from the 1954 work *Realities of American Foreign Policy*, no. **70**.)

1993

BOOKS

591. *Around the Cragged Hill: A Personal and Political Philosophy*. New York: Norton. 1992. 272p.

Kennan brings together his ideas on contemporary U.S. society and the international system; he is critical of much in the U.S.--from media addiction and lowest-common-denominator egalitarianism to foreign policy and policy-making--and offers suggestions for institutional reform.

(Excerpts reprinted nos. **595,597**.)

COMMENTARIES

592. "If TV Drives Foreign Policy, We're in Trouble." Letter to the editor. *New York Times*, 24 Oct. 1993, sec. 4, 14.

A reply to criticism of his Op-Ed article (no. **584**). Kennan defends his view and takes issue with the concept that television imparts enough information for informed decision-making.

593. "Introduction: The Balkan Crises, 1913 and 1993." In *The Other Balkan Wars, a 1913 Carnegie Endowment Inquiry in Retrospect*, with a new introduction and reflections on the present conflict by George F. Kennan, 3-16. Washington, D.C.: Carnegie Endowment for International Peace, 1993.

Gives a brief description of the background and circumstances of the 1913 Balkan wars, and of the Carnegie Commission report. Kennan notes similarities between that conflict and the one which began in 1993--indeed many of the problems stem from the same historical roots. The conflict will be resolved only when the Europeans and the international community find the political will to intervene. (Reprinted no. **596**.)

594. "Somalia, Through a Glass Darkly." *New York Times*, 30 Sept. 1993, 25.

The U.S. intervention in Somalia was a short-sighted and ineffectual action, which could not hope to cure long-term problems. This action, preceded by little congressional or public discussion, was largely an emotional response to the daily televised reports of suffering and starvation in Somalia. Such an emotional response leaves no room for purposeful diplomacy.

REPRINTS

595. "At Issue: Should the United States Curtail Immigration? Yes." *CQ Researcher* 3 (July 16, 1993): 617.

(Very brief excerpt from the work *Around the Cragged Hill*, no. **591**.)

596. "The Balkan Crisis 1913 and 1993." *New York Review of Books*, 15 July 1993, 3-7.

(Reprint of the commentary "Introduction: The Balkan Crises, 1913 and 1993," no. **593**.)

597. "George Kennan on U.S. Population Size and Immigration to the U.S." *Population and Development Review* 19 (June 1993): 417-421.

(Very brief excerpts from the work *Around the Cragged Hill*, no. **591**.)

598. "The Kennan Long Telegram, Moscow, February 22, 1946." In *Origins of the Cold War: The Novikov, Kennan, and Roberts "Long Telegrams" of 1946*, rev. ed., edited by Kenneth M. Jensen, 17-31. Washington, D. C.: United States Institute of Peace Press, 1993.

(Reprint of the document published in 1969, no. **350**. This publication is from a seminar conducted by the United States Institute For Peace and the Research Coordination Center of the Soviet Ministry of Foreign Affairs on the origins of the Cold War.)

1994

ARTICLES

599. "In Defense of Oppenheimer." *New York Review of Books*, 23 June 1994, 8.

Kennan contradicts the accusations made in a book by Pavel and Anatoli Sudoplatov, *Special Tasks: The Memoirs of an Unwanted Witness--A Soviet Spymaster*, that Robert Oppenheimer, director of the Los Alamos Project, was a Soviet spy. Kennan cites internal evidence from the book itself, as well as his own personal knowledge of Oppenheimer, and concludes with the hope that "the large body of historical evidence on these questions" now available will serve as testimony on this question, rather than this publication.

COMMENTARIES

600. "The Failure in our Success." *New York Times*, 14 Mar., 1994, 17.
Kennan reiterates his disagreement with the development of containment policy during the Cold War years, in which the U.S. and Western Europe sought unconditional surrender of the Soviets. Although it seems that this policy has had a spectacular success, the costs have been tremendous: unnecessary military expenditures, nuclear weapons proliferation, and forty years of Communist control in Eastern Europe. Kennan advises, for the future, that the U.S. look to principles in its foreign policy, rather than a new "Grand Strategy."
[From remarks at a celebration for Kennan's 90th birthday, held at the Council on Foreign Relations, New York City, Feb. 15.]

1995

ARTICLES

601. "From World War to Cold War." With John Lukacs. *American Heritage*, Dec. 1995, 42-67.
In the form of an exchange of letters with Lukacs, Kennan discusses the shift in U.S. policy toward the Soviets during 1945-1946 adding details to his analysis made in *Memoirs* (no. **306**) about the favorable reception of his "Long Telegram" (no. **350**) and his disagreements with U.S. policy toward Germany and negotiation with the Soviets. He disclaims any inconsistency between his views in the "Long Telegram" and his later criticisms of U.S. policy.

BOOK REVIEWS

602. "Witness to the Fall," review of *Autopsy on an Empire: The American Ambassador's Account of the Collapse of the Soviet Union*, by Jack F. Matlock, Jr. *New York Review of Books*, 16 Nov. 1995, 7-10.

1996

BOOKS

603. *At a Century's Ending: Reflections, 1982-1995*. New York: Norton, 1996. 351 p.
A collection of articles and lectures (some not previously published), in which Kennan talks about the Cold War, U.S. foreign relations, containment, and the arms race. In an original essay for this volume "The New Russia as Neighbor," he discusses Russia's relations with its bordering countries and Eastern Europe.

ORAL HISTORIES

604. "Interview With George F. Kennan, 19 February 1953, Room 5011, New State." (Transcript.) In *The Harry B. Price Interviews on the Marshall Plan.* 3 l. Harry S. Truman Library, Independence, Mo.

In very brief answers to questions, Kennan speaks about the Policy Planning Staff work on the Marshall Plan proposal. He touches on the point that the proposal was open to all European countries; the Soviet response; the move to make the plan a bipartisan effort; relations between the Executive and Legislative branches; and the success of the operation.

605. "Oral History Interview With George F. Kennan, March 23, 1965, Princeton N.J., by Louis Fischer for the John F. Kennedy Library." (Transcript) 141 l. John F. Kennedy Library, Boston, Mass.

Kennan talks about his Ambassadorship to Yugoslavia during the Kennedy Administration, his acquaintance with President Kennedy, and specifies criticisms and praise for Kennedy's handling of foreign policy issues. He discusses the Yugoslav reaction to the Cuban Missile Crisis and his own unsuccessful attempt to prevent Congressional denial of most-favored-nation trading status to Yugoslavia.

606. "Kennan, George F.," by Richard D. Challener. (Transcript.) In *The John Foster Dulles Oral History Collection.* Princeton University Library, 1967. 52p. Seeley G. Mudd Manuscript Library, Princeton University, Princeton, N.J.

Kennan discusses the Japanese Peace Treaty; Korea; controversy over the admission of the People's Republic of China to the U.N.; his opinions on Dulles' foreign policy; his official and personal relations with Dulles; and the McCarthy period.

ARCHIVAL COLLECTIONS

607. *C. Ben Wright Manuscript Collection.* George C. Marshall Research Foundation Library, Lexington, Va. 6 linear feet.
Research materials collected by Wright for his dissertation (no. **787**) and for an unpublished biography of Kennan co-authored by Wright and Larry Bland. Materials consist primarily of copied documents from the Policy Planning Staff records, *Foreign Relations of the United States* series, the Kennan papers at Princeton University, and secondary source materials by and about Kennan. There are also tape-recorded interviews with Kennan's colleagues and friends. The materials are open to interested scholars. An unpublished guide is in the Library. (Not seen.)

608. *George F. Kennan Papers.* Seeley G. Mudd Manuscript Library, Princeton University, Princeton, N.J. 17 linear feet publicly available.
Manuscripts, notes, articles, speeches, correspondence, clippings, and other papers of Kennan donated by him in 1968. The collection includes some official and semi-official papers relating to Kennan's tenure in the Foreign Service. Material is open to interested scholars. Photocopying is not permitted. An unpublished guide is in the Library.

609. National Archives, Washington, D.C.
Official documents and papers related to Kennan are found in numerous record groups; notable among these are Dept. of State Records: Personnel File 123, George F. Kennan; and Records of the Policy Planning Staff.
(Not seen.)

WORKS ABOUT KENNAN

610. Acheson, Dean. "The Illusion of Disengagement." *Foreign Affairs* 36 (Apr. 1958): 371-382.

A reply to Kennan's call for mutual Soviet-American withdrawal of forces from Europe (the Reith Lectures, no. **123**). Acheson vigorously defends the policy of strengthening NATO and West Germany as the best way to pull Eastern Europe into the West's orbit. Disengagement is tantamount to isolationism.

611. ______. "Text of Acheson's Reply to Kennan." *New York Times*, 12 Jan. 1958, 25.

Acheson responds to Kennan's Reith Lectures (especially nos. **123-124**), attacking his proposal for withdrawal of forces from Europe, and making it clear that this is not a position of the Democratic party. Such a move would make it impossible for Europe to "withstand Soviet pressures;" Kennan "has never grasped the realities of power."

612. Ascoli, Max. "George Kennan Updates His Diplomacy." *Reporter*, 23 Jan. 1958, 17-20.

Commends Kennan for clarifying the "inescabable implications" of U.S. foreign policy, and for trying to point the way to change in his Reith Lectures (nos. **121-126**). Nevertheless, Kennan's proposals for disengagement outline a world "even more frightening than the one we live in."

613. Atkinson, Brooks. "America's Global Planner." *New York Times Magazine*, 13 July 1947, 9, 32+.

A profile of Kennan just before he takes charge of the Policy Planning Staff, outlining Kennan's background, policy views, and the functions the PPS will have. If the PPS had been in existence at the time, the Truman Doctrine "might have had a more general and positive character in the public mind." Kennan defines differences between "liberal and totalitarian concepts," rather than between democracy and communism, and he sees possibilities for coexistence.

614. Barnet, Richard J. "A Balance Sheet: Lippmann, Kennan, and the Cold War." *Diplomatic History* 16 (spring 1992): 302-311.

Barnet cites the "contemporary relevance" of the debate between Walter Lippmann and Kennan on containment policy after World War II, as the U.S. again faces crucial changes in foreign affairs with the end of the Cold War. He reviews their arguments on the U.S. approach to the Soviet Union and reasons why a military policy was taken. Lippmann advocated diplomacy, while Kennan advocated containment. Kennan's views in the "X" article (no. **2**) were misinterpreted, and his analyses of the weaknesses of the Soviet state were ignored. Lippmann's prognosis that the U.S. would not have the staying-power for containment was not borne out, while Kennan's analysis of the Soviet Union has been vindicated. But if on the surface the balance sheet is in Kennan's favor, Lippmann did foresee the debilitating political and economic effects of the protracted Cold War and the problems of the U.S. as it arrives at a new crossroads in international affairs.

615. Bernstein, Barton J. "Containment." In *The Encyclopedia of American Foreign Policy: Studies of the Principal Movements and Ideas*, vol. 1, edited by Alexander DeConde, 191-203. New York: Charles Scribner's Sons, 1978.

Discusses the origins of the "X" article (no. **2**), interpretations of what Kennan meant, and criticisms of containment policy, including Kennan's own quarrel with the policy as it was carried out by Truman and Acheson.

616. Blumenfeld, Yorick. "New Wisdom, New Hope." *Vogue*, Jan. 1983, 206+.

A portrait of Kennan as a man of principle and reason, who is passionately outspoken in his opposition to U.S. nuclear policies. Blumenfeld briefly sketches Kennan's disagreements with U.S. policies and his regret at the politicization of foreign policy. Nevertheless, the public debate over nuclear weapons is "most significant . . . in any democratic society." He outlines Kennan's prescriptions for nuclear weapons reduction.

617. Brinkley, Douglas. "Kennan-Acheson: The Disengagement Debate." *Atlantic Community Quarterly* 25 (winter 1988/1989): 413-425.

Details the disagreement between Kennan and Acheson over disengagement (proposed by Kennan in the Reith Lectures, nos. **123-124**). Acheson spoke out against Kennan's proposal not only to tell the Europeans that Kennan's views were not official Democratic Party policy, and to defend his own policies under Truman, but also to insure that these policies continue and that the U.S. maintain a strong military presence in Europe. Kennan's concern was that a divided Europe was in the long run unhealthy. Brinkley calls the exchange "the opening salvo in a debate about American policy in the nuclear age."

618. Brown, Benjamin H. "Kennanland Revisited: In Search of a U.S. Foreign Policy." Parts 1 and 2. *New Leader*, 19 Sept. 1955, 13-16; 26 Sept. 1955, 16-19.

Brown argues that Kennan's realist critique of U.S. foreign policy discounts U.S. abilities for world leadership and the importance of the U.N. Kennan relies too much on "realism and power" without considering safeguards against the misuse of power. Kennan's view that morality can properly inform method but not purposes is a dangerous distinction. The U.S. must establish legitimacy in its actions; this will come from collective leadership, as, for example, in the Korean War.

619. Campbell, Craig. "George F. Kennan, American Diplomat and Historian." In *The Cold War, 1945-1991*, edited by Benjamin Frankel, foreword by Townsend Hoopes, v.1, *Leaders and Other Important Figures in the United States and Western Europe*, 251-

255. Detroit: Gale Research, 1992.
A biographical sketch covering the highlights of Kennan's career in the Foreign Service, the publication of the "Long Telegram" (no. **350**) and the "X" article (no. **2**), Kennan's change of emphasis in containment policy, his elitism, and criticism of U.S. nuclear strategy.

620. Carleton, William G. "Brain Trusters of American Foreign Policy." *World Politics* 7 (July 1955): 627-639.
An essay review of three books from former Policy Planning Staff personnel: Kennan's *Realities of American Foreign Policy* (no. **70**), Charles B. Marshall's *The Limits of American Foreign Policy* and Louis Halle's *Civilization and Foreign Policy*, in which Carleton analyzes Kennan's views on international relations and the Soviet Union. While Carleton praises Kennan's stance on cooperation with allies, he criticizes all three authors for failing "to integrate the gigantic social revolutions of the 20th century" with international relations.

621. Chalberg, John C. "George Kennan, Realist as Moralist." *Reviews in American History* 17 (Sept. 1989): 482-500.
An analysis of Kennan's historical interpretations in *American Diplomacy* (no. **525**), his realism, and changes in perspective from the 1950s. At that time, Kennan's realism was designed as an alternative to both Wilsonian messianism and isolationism. An unexpected and "subtle challenge came from the 'ultra realists,' who married Wilsonianism and power politics." In the 1950s Kennan had doubts that democracy was compatible with a rational foreign policy, but Chalberg points out that by the 1960s he "relied on the democratic process to obtain a hearing for his views" which were not in the mainstream of political thought.

622. ______. "Revealing Kennan: His Words and Silences." *Review of Politics* 52 (spring 1990): 298-304.
A review of *Sketches From a Life* (no. **564**), which also draws on Kennan's previous writings to characterize his thought. Chalberg finds that Kennan reveals little in *Sketches* apart from his distaste for, and even despair of, 20th-Century American culture.

623. Coffey, John W. "George F. Kennan and the Ambiguities of Realism." *South Atlantic Quarterly* 73 (spring 1974): 184-198.
Reviews the genesis of the "Long Telegram" (no. **350**) and the controversy surrounding the "X" article (no. **2**). Coffey says Kennan was never clear on the causes of the Cold War, and his analysis of Soviet intentions and the change in American-Russian relations also lacks clarity. (For a reprint of this and the next article, see John W. Coffey, *Political Realism In American Thought.* [Lewisburg, Penn.: Bucknell Univ. Press, 1977.])

624. ______. "The Political Realism of George F. Kennan." *Thought* 47 (summer 1972): 295-306.
Argues that Kennan's realism is less a theory than "a critique of . . . American democratic idealism." He takes issue with Kennan's statement that only the methods and not the purposes of governments can have moral content, and argues that this "selective" moralism is not evident in much of Kennan's other writings.

625. Cohen, Michael J. "Truman and the State Department: The Palestine Trusteeship

Proposal, March 1948." *Jewish Social Studies* 43 (spring 1981): 165-178.
Kennan figures in this argument within the Truman administration as an advocate against the forcible partition of Palestine, based on the strategic openings it could create for the Soviet Union in the Middle East.

626. Cohen, Warren I. "Acheson, His Advisers, and China, 1949-1950." In *Uncertain Years: Chinese-American Relations 1947-1950*, edited by Dorothy Borg and Waldo Heinrichs, 13-59. New York: Columbia Univ. Press, 1980.
In his analysis of Acheson's policy towards China, Cohen argues that Acheson initially heeded Kennan's advice for flexibility and measures to drive a wedge between Mao and the Soviets. Later events persuaded Acheson to abandon this policy; Cohen outlines relations between Acheson and Kennan at this time.

627. Combs, Jerald A. "The Compromise that Never Was: George Kennan, Paul Nitze, and the Issue of Conventional Deterrence in Europe, 1949-1952." *Diplomatic History* 15 (summer 1991): 361-386.
Compares the view of Kennan, Nitze (Kennan's successor on the Policy Planning Staff), and others on Soviet capabilities during this period, and the concurrent debate over how much of a military response the U.S. need make. Years later it was shown that Kennan was correct in calling U.S. estimates of Soviet military might exaggerated; nevertheless Kennan's advice was imprecise and ambiguous, vitiating its effect on the policy of militarization.

628. *Containing the Soviet Union: A Critique of U.S. Policy*, edited by Terry L. Deibel and John Lewis Gaddis. Washington, D.C.: Pergamon Brassey's International Defense Publishers, 1987. ix, 251p.
A collection of essays, most written for a conference honoring Kennan held at the National Defense University (including an essay by Kennan, no. **554**), bringing together critiques of containment policy from the realist school, and a look at the future of containment.

629. *Containment: Documents on American Policy and Strategy, 1945-1950*, edited by Thomas H. Etzold and John Lewis Gaddis. New York: Columbia Univ. Press, 1978. xii, 449p.
A collection of key documents on containment policy from the Joint Chiefs of Staff, the Policy Planning Staff, and the National Security Council, with commentary by the editors. Also included are Kennan's "Long Telegram" (no. **350**), the "X" article (no. **2**), a report from special counsel Clark Clifford to President Truman on relations with the Soviet Union, and an article by Gaddis on the conception and execution of containment policy.

630. Coogan, John W., and Michael H. Hunt. "Kennan and Containment: A Comment." *Society for Historians of American Foreign Relations Newsletter* 9 (Mar. 1978): 23-25.
A brief comment on Gaddis's 1977 article in *Foreign Affairs* (no. **642**) which questions his assessment that Kennan's containment policy was foresighted and consistent, citing recently released documents and new interpretations. They also call for more timely release of classified government documents and the "opening of Kennan's papers on an unrestricted and equitable basis." (See Gaddis's reply, no. **644**.)

631. Crossman, R. H. S. "The Strange Case of Mr. X--George Kennan." In *The Charm* *of Politics and Other Essays*, by R. H. S. Crossman, 128-133. London: Hamish Hamilton, 1958.

Comments on aspects of *American Diplomacy, 1900-1950* (no. **22**), and the persistence of the "legalism and moralism" in U.S. diplomacy which Kennan criticizes. Crossman argues that Kennan was just as utopian as Wilson was, in his day, in advocating change that could not occur under the political conditions of the time. Kennan's criticisms only served to "remove the moral inhibitions on power politics." (This essay was first published in *New Statesman and Nation* in 1952.)

632. Danchev, Alex. "Diplomacy's Wise Man?" *Wilson Quarterly*, autumn 1989, 104-106.

An essay review of Kennan's *Sketches From a Life* (no. **564**), Mayers's *George Kennan and the Dilemmas of U.S. Foreign Policy* (no. **699**), and Stephanson's *Kennan and the Art of Foreign Policy* (no. **742**), in which Danchev comments briefly on Kennan's influence and lack of influence, his realist philosophy, and the denouement of containment.

633. Davis, Reed. "George F. Kennan." In *Traditions and Values: American Diplomacy 1945 to the Present*, edited by Kenneth W. Thompson, 197-211. Lanham, Md.: University Press of America, 1984.

Davis presents Kennan's political philosophy as based, materially, in the contingency and flux of the modern world of nations; morally, in the alienation forcing men and nations to an unceasing reassessment of goals. Davis praises Kennan's dialectical approach, his recognition of the "organic character of historical reality," and his rejection of "single cause" analyses.

634. *Decline of the West? George F. Kennan and His Critics*, edited by Martin F. Herz. Washington, D.C.: Ethics and Public Policy Center, Georgetown Univ., 1978. xvi, 173p.

An interview and excerpts from previously published articles, in which Kennan and other historians and political scientists--Hugh Seton-Watson, Richard Pipes, Eugene Rostow, John Lewis Gaddis, Michael Novak, Seymour Weiss, Edward Luttwak and Eduard Mark--discuss U.S. policy toward the Soviets from widely different viewpoints.

(See, for some individual articles, nos. **423,429,434,446,642,692,695,718,724,733**.)

635. Donovan, John C. "Containment: The New American Strategic-Political Doctrine, 1947." In *The Cold Warriors: A Policy-Making Elite*, by John C. Donovan, 58-80. Lexington, Mass.: D. C. Heath, 1974.

Examines the origins of containment doctine, the history of the "X" article (no. **2**) and the "Long Telegram" (no. **350**), and briefly outlines Kennan's and Acheson's disagreements over policy.

636. Downey, Betsy. "In Which 'Mr. X' Goes to Asia: George Frost Kennan and Containment in China and Korea: 1947-1950." *Mid-America* 72 (1990): 71-89.

Kennan's policy recommendations on China and Korea during this period were more flexible than critics have charged. He did draw the line for containment at mainland China, but was not in favor of propping up Chiang Kai-shek. He was critical of taking the war in Korea above the 38th parallel, and recommended negotiation after American reverses there. It was the Korean War that ultimately brought about a militant policy in China and Korea.

637. Eddy, W. H. C."Kennan's Estimates of Soviet Policy." *Australian Outlook*, June 1958, 43-51.

Kennan's evident acceptance of coexistence in the first two Reith Lectures (nos. **121-122**) shows a lack of understanding of the communists, would yield too much, and "debase" Western thinking.

638. *Encounters with Kennan: The Great Debate*. Introduction by Daniel P. Moynihan. London: F. Cass, 1979. xi, 218p.

A collection of reprints, articles by and about Kennan, from *Encounter* between 1960 and 1978, arguing the question whether Kennan has retreated from the containment policy, and what U.S. policy toward the Soviet Union should be. Interviews with Melvin J. Lasky and George Urban; articles about Kennan by Leopold Labedz, Richard Lowenthal, Michael Novak, Richard Pipes, and Hugh Seton-Watson. (See individual articles nos. **187,423,443,449,680,710,718,733**.)

639. Evans, M. Stanton. "The Liberal Against Himself." *National Review*, 22 Dec. 1956, 11-13.

Criticizes Kennan for not denouncing communism in an interview with Joseph Alsop on the Hungarian uprising in 1956 (no. **106**) and faults Kennan for contradicting himself in various statements on Soviet domination of Eastern Europe.

640. Feighan, Michael. "The Kennan Fables." *Ukrainian Quarterly* 14 (Mar. 1958): 10-17.

Takes issue with Kennan's statements in the Reith Lectures (no. **123**) as to the Soviets' economic success and his proposals for a united Germany. The Russians are not as benign as Kennan thinks and it would be "a disservice to Anglo-American relations" if his statements are given credibility in Britain.

641. [*Foreign Affairs*.] "Containment 40 Years Later." *Foreign Affairs* 65 (1987): 827-890.

On the anniversary of the "X" article (no. **2**), reviews the history of the article, reprints the article and Lippmann's criticism of it, and includes an essay "On Ending the Cold War" by W. W. Rostow.
(For Kennan article included here, see no. **545**.)

642. Gaddis, John Lewis. "Containment: A Reassessment." *Foreign Affairs* 55 (July 1977): 873-887.

An analysis of the "X" article (no. **2**), which supports Kennan's own claim that his expression of containment was quite different from the way the policy was implemented.
(Reprinted in no. **634**.)

643. ______. "Containment: Its Past and Future." *International Security* 5 (1981): 74-102.

Kennan's principles of containment are briefly reviewed in this analysis of the structure of Soviet-American relations in the Cold War, and the permutations of containment. Gaddis outlines characteristics for a "new containment."

644. ______. "Kennan and Containment: A Reply." *Society for Historians of American Foreign Relations Newsletter* 9 (1978): 26-27.

Replies to the comment by Coogan and Hunt (no. **630**.) defending his interpretation of overall consistency in Kennan's views on containment. Gaddis shares the authors' concern about the availability of papers and documents.

645. ______. *The Long Peace, Inquiries Into the History of the Cold War*. New York: Oxford Univ. Press, 1987. ix, 332p.

In the course of this historical analysis of important themes and questions of the Cold War and its characteristics, Gaddis looks at Kennan's thought and influence on policies toward the Soviet Union and its weaknesses, international communism, balance of power and spheres of influence, European integration, Eastern Europe, and nuclear weapons.

646. ______. "Morality and the Cold War." In *Ethics and International Relations*, edited with an introduction by Kenneth W. Thompson, 109-126. New Brunswick, N.J.: Transaction Books, 1985. (Ethics in foreign policy, v. 2)

In this examination of whether U.S. Cold War policy was consistent with its moral standards, Gaddis touches on Kennan's views on some troubling issues in the debate--covert activities, intervention, and nuclear weapons policy.

647. ______. *Strategies of Containment: A Critical Appraisal of Postwar American National Security Policy*. New York: Oxford Univ. Press, 1982. xi, 432p.

A history of U.S. containment through 1979, focusing on military and political policies. In a chapter analyzing Kennan's formulations of containment, Gaddis outlines Kennan's thought on the Soviets as adversaries: his emphasis on the U.S. and the West restoring self-confidence and setting an example, his specification of areas of vital interest, his preference for a particularist rather than a universalist policy, his balancing of military and political containment, and his views on encouraging "Titoist" tendencies. Kennan looked to the inevitable breakup of international communism from its own self-destructive imperialism; containment was a positive policy for the West.

648. Gardner, Lloyd C. "American Foreign Policy, 1900-1921: A Second Look at the Realist Critique of *American Diplomacy*." In *Towards a New Past: Dissenting Essays in American History*, edited by Barton Bernstein, 202-231. New York: Pantheon, 1968.

Argues that Kennan's critique of diplomacy of this time is flawed. Rather than being "idealist," the Open Door policies, and later Woodrow Wilson's policies were aimed at making the U.S. economically competitive, extending its influence, and extending democracy and stability. The realist critique, unfortunately, has been used as a justification for an elitist rather than a "popular" diplomacy and it has served as a rationale for extending commitments abroad, rather than narrowing them.

649. ______. "James V. Forrestal and George F. Kennan: Will the Real 'Mr. X' Please Stand Up?" In *Architects of Illusion: Men and Ideas in American Foreign Policy, 1941-1949*, by Lloyd C. Gardner, 270-300. Chicago: Quadrangle Books, 1970.

Gardner sees Kennan taking a harder line on containment in his "X" article (no. **2**) than he later admits in his *Memoirs* (no. **306**), and interprets this as partly the influence of Forrestal and partly an "overreaction" to what he felt was Roosevelt's insufficient appreciation of Soviet venality.

650. Gati, Charles, ed. *Caging the Bear: Containment and the Cold War*. Indianapolis:

Bobbs Merrill, 1974. xxvi, 228p.

A collection of articles on containment, including a reprint of Gati's own article in *Foreign Policy* (no. **757**), in which he concludes Kennan did indicate global containment, despite his later disclaimers. With an interview with Kennan, (no. **383**) and a reprint of the "X" article (no. **2**).

651. Gellman, Barton. *Contending with Kennan: Toward a Philosophy of American Power*. New York: Praeger, 1984. xvii, 172p.

Synthesizes Kennan's thoughts on morality, the national interest, democracy, and foreign policy, bringing out continuities and contradictions.

652. Good, Robert C. "The National Interest and Political Realism, Niebuhr's 'Debate' with Morgenthau and Kennan." *Journal of Politics* 22 (Nov. 1960): 597-619.

Compares and contrasts Niebuhr's concept of the national interest with Kennan's and Morgenthau's. Kennan does not see international relations governed by the same norms or principles of morality as individual behavior. Good defines Kennan's position as "humane relativism."

653. Grann, David. "Kennan at 90 Still in Seach of Mr. X." *Fletcher Forum of World Affairs* 18 (summer/fall 1994): 151-167.

Grann synthesizes Kennan's thinking on international relations with analyses of his major writings including the "Long Telegram" (no. **350**), the "X" article (no. **2**), the Reith Lectures (nos. **121-126**), and *The Cloud of Danger* (no. **431**). Grann sees Kennan as a realist in all these writings, despite criticisms to the contrary. The discontinuity came not in Kennan's realism, but in his growing pessimism at the fragmentation of purpose in U.S. society. Kennan's containment policy was misunderstood, but his realism is flawed in his assessment of the ability of a democracy to conduct foreign affairs, and in his assumption that "prudence and principle are mutually exclusive."

654. Greenwood, Sean. "Frank Roberts and the 'Other' Long Telegram: The View from the British Embassy in Moscow, March 1946." *Journal of Contemporary History* 25 (Jan. 1990): 103-122.

Compares a message written at about the same time as the "Long Telegram" (no. **350**) from Kennan's counterpart at the British Embassy in Moscow, Frank Roberts, and finds many similarities of viewpoint.

655. Halle, Louis J. "George Kennan and the Common Mind." *Virginia Quarterly Review* 45 (winter 1969): 46-57.

Briefly characterizes Kennan's understanding of international relations and his sensitivity and intelligence as a Russian expert in the State Department. Halle analyzes points of divergence with Acheson and Truman over containment policy.

656. ______. "The World of George Kennan." *New Republic*, 7 Aug. 1961, 21-23.

An overview of Kennan's philosophy, with reference specifically to *Russia and the West Under Lenin and Stalin* (no. **206**). Although Kennan's world is one of "good and evil," he places a greater emphasis on personality over ideology. In Kennan's view, there are "no absolute . . . differences between Russian humanity and . . . American humanity." Kennan thus is distinguished from other Kremlinologists.

657. Harper, John Lamberton. *American Visions of Europe: Franklin D. Roosevelt,*

George F. Kennan and Dean G. Acheson. Cambridge: Cambridge Univ. Press, 1994. xi, 378p.

A close analysis of Kennan's views on postwar policy in Europe, comparing them to those of Roosevelt and Acheson. Harper sees Kennan favoring an autonomous, united Europe (and a united Germany). He contrasts this view to Roosevelt's vision of a Europe of independent non-imperialist countries and Acheson's view of Europe under the aegis and protection of the U.S. Harper's method, incorporating biographical detail to explain these three concepts of Europe, contributes to an understanding of Kennan in his time.

658. ______. "Friends not Allies: George F. Kennan and Charles E. Bohlen." *World Policy Journal* 12 (summer 1995): 77-88.

This is a revealing analysis of Kennan's alternatives to cold war policies, based on an exploration of the differences in outlook of these two prominent Soviet experts. Both Kennan and Bohlen held similar views as to Soviet intentions and capabilities, but diverged on questions of diplomacy and tactics, and in their relation to the machinery of U.S. policy. Their differences centered on U.S. policies in Europe, with Bohlen favoring a strong western alliance, which Kennan felt would hurt chances for European unification. Their differing reactions toward NSC68 in 1950 are shown to reflect the way their similar factual analyses led to divergent policy preferences.

659. Harrington, Daniel F. "Kennan, Bohlen, and the Riga Axioms." *Diplomatic History* 2 (1978): 423-437.

Defends Kennan and Bohlen against the argument that they had a major part in development of a militaristic containment policy.

660. Herald, George W. "Mister X in Quest of Peace." *United Nations World*, Mar. 1952, 17-20.

A profile of Kennan before he assumes the post of ambassador to the Soviet Union, outlining his diplomatic background, his understanding of Soviet diplomacy, and what he hopes to achieve.

661. Herken, Gregg. "The Great Foreign Policy Fight." *American Heritage*, Apr./May 1986, 65-80.

Compares the views and careers of Kennan and Paul Nitze. Their disagreements centered on the importance of militarization of U.S. policy and analysis of Soviet aims. While Nitze's views gained favor in official Washington from the late 1940s, Kennan became a critic of U.S. policy and deplored reliance on nuclear weapons. Later, Kennan favored the SALT talks, which Nitze opposed. Nevertheless, the two maintained a mutual respect and remained friends.

662. Hillman, Eugene. "Doing Evil for a Good Cause." *America*, 10 May 1986, 379-382.

Attacks Kennan, Reinhold Niebuhr, and Hans J. Morgenthau, for their influence in bringing about moral degeneracy in foreign affairs. Referring to Kennan's article in *Foreign Affairs* (no. **545**), Hillman disputes the idea of a separate morality for individuals and the state; and he finds that Kennan now sees the need for moral standards in foreign policy.

663. Hixson, Walter L. "Containment on the Perimeter: George F. Kennan and

Vietnam." *Diplomatic History* 12 (1988): 149-163.

Traces a change in Kennan's thinking from the immediate postwar period, when he inclined towards global containment including South Vietnam, to the mid-1960s, by which time Kennan had become a critic of U.S. foreign policy and was advocating withdrawal from South Vietnam.

664. ______. *George F. Kennan: Cold War Iconoclast.* New York: Columbia Univ. Press, 1983. xiii, 381p.

A full-length intellectual biography, tracing Kennan's thought and influence in foreign affairs from within and outside the government. As against others, Hixson sees change, over the years, in Kennan's position on containment. He sees Kennan's greatest contribution in his ceaseless questioning and probing of ideas and in the consequent evolution of his thinking on the Cold War. (See also his dissertation, no. **773**.)

665. Hoffmann, Stanley. "Mr. X." *New Republic*, 2 Oct. 1989, 35-38.

Reviewing Kennan's *Sketches from a Life* (no. **564**), Mayers's *George Kennan and the Dilemmas of U.S. Foreign Policy* (no. **699**), Stephanson's *Kennan and the Art of Foreign Policy* (no. **742**), and Hixson's *George F. Kennan: Cold War Iconoclast* (no. **664**), Hoffmann assesses Kennan's strengths and idiosyncracies as a thinker. The basic concepts behind containment were correct. Kennan's conservatism is a complex blend of his "genuine feeling for nature and of the synthetic idealization of a mythical past," to which might be traced his elitism. But Kennan's "concern for the fragility of civilization" is another strength.

666. Hollander, Paul. "The Two Faces of George Kennan: From Containment to 'Understanding'." *Policy Review* 33 (summer 1985): 28-34.

Kennan has moved from advocating a firm response to the Soviets to accommodation. Hollander deplores Kennan making moral judgements about the U.S. but not the Soviets, and discusses reasons for this, among them exaggerated concern for environmental disaster. Despite Kennan's admitted preference for authoritarianism and opposition to the New Left in the 1960s, his alienation and antipathy to U.S. culture makes him not a neoconservative but more appreciative of the Soviets.

667. Hollist, W. Ladd. "War, Peace, and Arms Control: A Review Essay." *Brigham Young University Studies* 25 (winter 1985): 167-174.

Arms control was considered to be essential in the 1960s and 1970s, but fell out of favor in the Reagan administration. The three works under review, Kennan's *Nuclear Delusion* (no. **495a**), the article "The President's Choice: Star Wars or Arms Control, by Kennan with Robert McNamara, Gerard Smith, and McGeorge Bundy (no. **535**), and Strobe Talbott's *Deadly Gambit: The Reagan Administration and the Stalemate in Nuclear Arms Control*, are convincing in advocating arms control negotiations. Hollist mentions Kennan's early and continuing endorsement of control of nuclear weapons.

668. Hunt, Michael. *Ideology and U.S. Foreign Policy.* New Haven: Yale Univ. Press, 1987. 273p.

In his opening section Hunt contrasts Kennan's anti-ideological critique of a naive legalistic and moralistic American foreign policy with that of William Appleman Williams, who finds the same policies shrewd and ideologically driven. Hunt finds

Kennan's realism an ideology it itself.

669. Inglis, Fred. "The Diplomat--George Kennan." In *The Cruel Peace, Everyday Life in the Cold War*, by Fred Inglis, 87-95. New York: Basic Books, 1991.
A brief sketch of Kennan's career, influence, and character. Inglis sees Kennan as a voice against Cold War militarization (from the Reith Lectures, (nos. **121-126** and subsequent writings) whose ideas are characterized by the "noble ideals of public duty, diplomatic probity, [and] personal faithfulness."

670. Isaacson, Walter, and Evan Thomas. *The Wise Men: Six Friends and the World They Made: Acheson, Bohlen, Harriman, Kennan, Lovett, McCloy*. New York: Simon and Schuster, 1986. 853p.
A collective biography of policy-makers in administrations from Truman to Johnson, which puts the forging of the postwar foreign policy consensus in a historical and personal context.

671. Kalb, Marvin. "The Vital Interests of Mr. Kennan." *New York Times Magazine*, 27 Mar. 1966, 30-31+.
A profile of Kennan a month after his testimony in Senate hearings, in which he proposed "liquidation" of the U.S. position in Vietnam (see no. **289**). Kalb summarizes Kennan's ideas on foreign policy in general, areas he counts as vital interests, his view that communism itself is not a threat in underdeveloped countries, and the need for control of nuclear weapons.

672. Kateb, George. "George F. Kennan: The Heart of a Diplomat." *Commentary*, Jan. 1968, 21-26.
In this essay review of Kennan's *Memoirs, 1925-1950* (no. **306**), with references to *American Diplomacy, 1900-1950* (no. **22**) and volume 1 of *Soviet-American Relations, 1917-1920* (no. **97**), Kateb explores Kennan's feelings as an exile from U.S. civilization, and points to his moralism which is in contradiction to his realism. Kateb concludes that moralism and "decency" have brought Kennan to speak out against the Vietnam War.

673. Kazin, Alfred. "Man of State." *New York Review of Books*, 2 Nov. 1972, 3.
In a review of *Memoirs, 1950-1963* (no. **306**) Kazin characterizes Kennan as cultivated and knowledgeable but removed from contemporary American life. Kennan's "failures" are overblown in his autobiography, and come from his inability to play the political game. Kazin says Kennan suffers "the futility of wanting to be nothing but an insider--while thinking like an outsider."

674. ______. "Solitary Expert: The Case of George F. Kennan." *Atlantic Monthly*, Jan. 1968, 59-67.
Reviews Kennan's *Memoirs, 1925-1950* presenting Kennan's views on postwar policy, similarities in the Russian and American peoples, and his dislike of contemporary American society. Kazin remarks on Kennan's complexity, "to love Russia itself so much, and yet never to grant anything to the Bolshevik Revolution, to despise Americans in their military-government compounds abroad . . . yet all the while angrily to blame them for not being politically more intelligent. These are some of the views that make Kennan the extraordinary figure he is."

675. King, James E., Jr. "Kennanism and Disengagement." *New Republic*, 7 Apr. 1958,

12-16.

Kennan's proposals on disengagement are misguided at this time: the Soviets are not looking for bargaining. NATO would be weakened by a withdrawal of forces from Germany.

676. Kissinger, Henry. "Reflections on Containment." *Foreign Affairs* 73 (May/June 1994): 113-130.

An overview of containment policy and its ambiguities. Kissinger briefly reviews the origins of containment in Kennan's "X" article (no. **2**), which accurately predicted the collapse of the Soviet Union, Clark Clifford's memorandum, and President Truman's contributions. He outlines criticism, from Walter Lippmann's realist position, to Prime Minister Churchill's reluctance to postpone negotiations, and Henry Wallace's moral objections. Containment was criticized both for being too passive and too interventionist. It was at once "hard-headed and idealistic" and the U.S. was caught up in its ambiguities as it was drawn into questionable causes in pursuit of moral perfection.

677. Knight, Jonathan. "George Frost Kennan and the Study of American Foreign Policy: Some Critical Comments." *Western Political Quarterly* 20 (Mar. 1967): 149-160.

Analyzes Kennan's criticisms of the conduct of foreign policy, and is critical of his use of abstractions.

678. Korovin, Y. "A Distorted View of Peaceful Coexistence." *International Affairs* (Moscow), Feb. 1960, 69-74.

A refutation of Kennan's statements in the *Foreign Affairs* article "Peaceful Co-existence, A Western View" (no. **189**). Lenin never advocated interference in the internal affairs of other countries, capitalism has not changed beyond recognition in capitalist countries, and the satellite countries are not coerced by Moscow. Kennan is wrong to discount world trade as a force for peace, and Soviet foreign policy is not aggressive.

679. Kovel, Joel. "George Kennan: Anticommunism from the Mountaintop." In *Red Hunting in the Promised Land: Anti-communism and the Making of America*, by Joel Kovel, 39-63. New York: Basic Books, 1994.

Although Kennan was a critic of anti-communism, he nevertheless was a major contributor to anti-communist doctrine. In the "Long Telegram" (no. **350**) and subsequent writings, he excluded the Soviets from the "moral universe" inhabited by U.S. diplomacy. Kennan's brand of "elite anticommunism" cloaked "demonization of communism and naked economic interests beneath Puritan ideals."

680. Labedz, Leopold. "The Two Minds of George Kennan: How to Un-Learn From Experience." *Encounter*, Apr. 1978, 78-86.

Attacks the "ambiguities and contradictions" Kennan uses in arguments about containment policy. Kennan is mistaken about Soviet expansionism and intentions now, though he was correct in 1946 and 1947. (Reprinted in no. **638**.)

681. Lasch, Christopher. "Realism as a Critique of American Diplomacy." In *The World of Nations: Reflections on American History, Politics and Culture*, by Christopher Lasch, 205-215. New York: Alfred A. Knopf, 1973.

Realist criticism of American foriegn policy, expressed by Kennan and by Walter Lippmann, misses the point of that policy's failures. The history of World War I diplomacy, and of Woodrow Wilson's policies, is not an example of "idealism" over "self-interest," as the realists would have it. Rather, Wilson's policies were based on the national interest as he saw it, and, like most politicians, he unconsciously translated "self-interest . . . into the language of high idealism." The real problem with U.S. policy was not that Americans were pursuing idealist goals, but that that the "moral judgements they made were so shallow." (First published in *The Nation*, Nov. 24, 1962.)

682. Lasky, Melvin J., ed. *The West, the Atom, and Russia: A Round Table Discussion of the Views of George F. Kennan; Including a Reply by George Kennan*. Paris: Congress for Cultural Freedom, 1958. 68p.

(See no. **143** for annotation. See also no. **187**.)

683. Layne, Christopher. "The Real Conservative Agenda." *Foreign Policy* 61 (winter 1985/86): 73-93.

Arguing that the Reagan Doctrine of global containment will drain resources and fail to revive U.S. hegemony, Layne identifies Kennan as a "real conservative" who favors economically viable selective containment.

684. ______. "Super Power Disengagement." *Foreign Policy* 77 (winter 1989/1990): 17-40.

Reviews the controversy over disengagement in the late 1940s, and finds the questions Kennan raised then in regard to a European security force relevant to the situation in the late 1980s.

685. Leffler, Melvyn P. "Was the Cold War Necessary?" *Diplomatic History* 15 (spring 1991): 265-275.

A review of Hixson's *George F. Kennan: Cold War Iconoclast* (no. **664**) and Stephanson's *Kennan and the Art of Foreign Policy* (no. **742**). Leffler notes differing approaches but similiarities in themes of the two works: Kennan's support for an "ideological-political war against the Soviet Union" and his support for a militaristic containment policy. Both authors question the "realism" of containment, and the need for militarization and globalization of the Cold War.

686. Lerner, Max. "Mr. X, Mr. L, and Mr. S." In *Actions and Passions*, by Max Lerner, 301-304. New York: Simon and Schuster, 1949.

A commentary on the "X" article (no. **2**) and Lippmann's criticisms (no. **688**). Lerner sees Kennan's view favoring an overthrow of a vulnerable Soviet Union, while Lippmann favors better relations and more trade to bring about peace. In spite of the U.S. shift of emphasis from the Truman Doctrine to the Marshall Plan, the underlying philosophy remains militaristic; it would be better to favor democratic reconstruction.

687. Lichtheim, George. "The Private Philosophy." In *Collected Essays*, by George Lichtheim, 128-133. New York: Viking Press, 1973.

In an essay comparing the ideas expressed by Walter Lippmann in his *The Public Philosophy* and Kennan in *Realities of American Foreign Policy* (no. **70**) concerning the abilities of democratic states to pursue foreign policies and the value of moralism, Lichtheim argues that "on the general attitude appropriate to a pluralist society Mr. Kennan is sounder than Mr. Lippmann."

688. Lippmann, Walter. *The Cold War: A Study of U.S. Foreign Policy*. New York: Harper, 1972. xvii, 81p.

Originally published in 1947 in answer to the "X" article (no. **2**), Lippman describes containment as a "strategic monstrosity," which would severely tax the resources of the U.S. (An excerpt appears in *Foreign Affairs* 65 (spring 1987): 869-884.)

689. ______. "Mr. Kennan and Reappraisal." *Atlantic Monthly*, Apr. 1958, 33-37.

A favorable comment on Kennan's proposals for disengagement in the Reith Lectures. Lippmann sees his proposals offering a real choice in policy direction. Although he disagrees with some specifics of Kennan's proposals, they have provided an opportunity for a reexamination that is much needed.

690. Lowenthal, Richard. "What Kennan Represents." *New Republic*, 10 Feb. 1958, 6-7.

A reply to an editorial (Jan. 20), in which Lowenthal explains the European reaction to Kennan's position on disengagement and interprets the Kennan-Acheson debate as an argument "about how best to conduct the Cold War, not about whether the Cold War is necessary."

691. Lukacs, John. "The Soviet State at 65." *Foreign Affairs* 65 (fall 1986): 21-36.

In the course of a review of Soviet history since the Revolution, Lukacs calls Kennan's expression of containment "judicious" and judges that the language of Acheson and the Truman Doctrine was "not at all comparable."

692. Luttwak, Edward N. "The Strange Case of George F. Kennan: From Containment to Isolationism." *Commentary*, Nov. 1977, 30-35.

A critical review essay of *The Cloud of Danger* (no. **431**). Luttwak argues that Kennan's view of the U.S. as "ill-suited to the task of conducting a foreign policy of global dimensions" is harmfully isolationist and ignores U.S. responsibilities. Kennan does not appreciate the role of military power in foreign policy. (Reprinted in no. **634**.)

693. MacDougal, Myres S. "Law and Power." *American Journal of International Law* 46 (Jan. 1952): 102-114.

Reviewing Kennan's *American Diplomacy, 1900-1950* (no. **22**), and Hans Morgenthau's *In Defense of the National Interest*, MacDougal finds a misconception of morality and power in both works. He argues against Kennan's interpretations of decision-making in connection with the "legalism and moralism" of U.S. policy, and he is critical of Kennan's lack of faith in the U.N. and other alliances.

694. McLellan, David S. "Who Fathered Containment? A Discussion." *International Studies Quarterly* 17 (June 1973): 205-226.

An answer to the Powers article (no. **721**), argues that containment was practised by Truman before either Kennan's "Long Telegram" or Clark Clifford's memorandum. It arose from "concrete situations" rather than the "theoretical formulations of the planners."

695. Mark, Eduard. "The Question of Containment: A Reply to John Lewis Gaddis." *Foreign Affairs* 56 (Jan. 1978): 428-441.

Argues, in response to an article by Gaddis in an earlier issue, that the military component of containment as originally expressed by Kennan was greater than Kennan now admits. Followed by a rebuttal from Gaddis. Also rebutted by Kennan in this issue, see no. **442**. (Reprinted in no. **634**.)

696. Mayers, David. "Containment and the Primacy of Diplomacy: George Kennan's Views, 1947-1948." *International Security* 11 (1986): 124-162.

A study of the background of the "X" article (no. **2**) and of what Kennan meant by containment at the time. Mayers concludes that, for Kennan, the military component was as important as the political and economic; Kennan's concept of containment was more subtle than many of his critics contend.

697. ______. "Diplomacy and the Politics of Amelioration: The Thought of George Kennan." *Virginia Quarterly Review* 67 (spring 1991): 189-213.

Kennan's thought on international relations is not neatly compartmentalized, although it fits most closely into the realist tradition, with its emphasis on gradual change over utopian goals, and on preserving a distinction between the morality of the individual and of the state. Mayers draws comparisons between Kennan and other realists. He also identifies distinctive characteristics in his thought indicative of a "conservative European tradition," such as Kennan's "romantic attachment to the past," his "dubious anti-democratic viewpoint," and his "concept of custodianship," contributing to his status as a political outsider. Nevertheless, Kennan has succeeded in trenchant analyses of U.S. foreign policy problems, and his concept of custodianship is of vital importance in the face of the challenge to avoid nuclear conflagration. (Cf. Mayers' biography of Kennan (no. **699**) for a slightly different form of this article.)

698. ______. "George F. Kennan." In *Statesmen Who Changed the World, A Bio-Bibliographical Dictionary of Diplomacy*, edited by Frank W. Thackeray and John E. Findling, 277-285. Westport, Conn.: Greenwood Press, 1993.

Briefly outlines Kennan's career in the Foreign Service, his development as a Soviet expert, and his later accomplishments as a scholar and commentator on international and domestic issues. Includes an annotated bibliography.

699. ______. *George Kennan and the Dilemmas of U.S. Foreign Policy*. New York: Oxford Univ. Press, 1988. xiv, 402p.

A full-length political and intellectual biography of Kennan as a diplomat, statesman, and scholar. Mayers emphasizes continuity over change in Kennan's stance on containment, and he finds strains of conservatism just as strong as realism in his thinking. He sees Kennan as being more effective as a critic than as an implementer of foreign policy.

700. ______. "George Kennan and the Soviet Union, 1933-1938: Perceptions of a Young Diplomat." *International History Review* 4 (Nov. 1983): 525-549.

Details Kennan's early career in the Soviet Union and shows these experiences were formative in his views of the basic differences and incompatibility between the U.S. and the U.S.S.R.

701. ______. "The Practitioner/Theorist in American Foreign Policy: George Kennan." In *Centerstage: American Diplomacy Since World War II*, edited by L. Carl Brown, 305-327. New York: Holmes & Meyer, 1990.

An essay on Kennan as a theorist, which traces some seemingly incongruous aspects of Kennan's thought. Mayers discusses his realism, conservatism, and ideas on democracy. Mayers is critical of some of Kennan's ideas, while commending his approach to international relations.

702. ______. "Soviet War Aims and the Grand Alliance: George Kennan's Views, 1944-1946." *Journal of Contemporary History* 21 (Jan. 1986): 57-79.

Explores in detail Kennan's attitudes toward the U.S.S.R. in this period. Kennan was skeptical of the Soviets as an ally during the war, in contrast to Roosevelt's policies; but Kennan's views were more sophisticated than his later critics allowed. Kennan favored balance-of-power and diplomacy, rather than reliance on the U.N. to keep international agreements. Mayers discusses the "Long Telegram" (no. **350**), and Kennan's rise within and outside the State Dept. as a Soviet expert.

703. ______. "Young Kennan's Criticisms and Recommendations." *Biography* 8 (1985): 227-247.

Drawing largely on unpublished manuscripts of Kennan's written in 1938 and 1942, Mayers details Kennan's early disenchantment with the U.S. political system and American society. Kennan was most critical of the influence of special interests; he recommended forging a political elite that would be free from particular interests, and he even contemplated constitutional change. Mayers traces recurrence of these themes in some of Kennan's later writings.

704. Messer, Robert L. "Paths Not Taken: The United States Department of State and Alternatives to Containment, 1945-1946." *Diplomatic History* 1 (1977): 297-319.

Outlines alternatives to the containment policy aired in the State Department prior to Kennan's "Long Telegram" (no. **350**), and offers reasons for the adoption of containment.

705. Miscamble, Wilson D. "Deciding to Divide Germany." *Diplomacy and Statecraft* 2 (1991): 294-320.

Details policy-making in 1947-1949 leading to the division of Germany. Miscamble argues that this was not a predetermined pursuit of containment policy but rather the result of "piecemeal and staggered" actions significantly influenced by the Europeans. Acheson seriously considered the alternative recommended by Kennan for withdrawal of Allied forces and German reunification until mid-1949. Kennan viewed the failure of his policy as a "fundamental defeat" for himself.

706. ______. *George F. Kennan and the Making of American Foreign Policy, 1947-1950.* Princeton, N.J.: Princeton Univ. Press, 1992. xvii, 419p.

Miscamble focuses on the role of the State Department's Policy Planning Staff, with Kennan as its director, in forging major postwar policies: the Marshall Plan; the formation of NATO; policy on Germany, Eastern Europe, China, Japan, and Korea; and the place of the hydrodgen bomb in U.S. strategy. Differences on these issues are explored in detail, and Miscamble sees their "working-out," rather than any single formula or doctrine, as the source of containment policy. Although many of Kennan's recommendations met with defeat, he played a central role in policy-making at this time. (See also this author's dissertation, no. **777**.)

707. ______. "George F. Kennan, the Policy Planning Staff, and the Origins of the Marshall Plan." *Mid-America* 62 (1980): 75-89.

Details the decision-making process and contributions from various individuals as well as the Policy Planning Staff in the development of the European Recovery Program from Apr.-Sept. 1947, and shows the important role played by Kennan and the PPS.

708. *Morality and Foreign Policy: Realpolitik Revisited*, edited by Kenneth M. Jensen and Elizabeth Faulkner. Washington, D.C.: United States Institute of Peace, 1991. xii, 80p.

Scholars in this symposium discuss the significance of Kennan's position on morality and foreign policy. The preface by Samuel W. Lewis suggests that Kennan reflects a Cold War era that has vanished. David Little argues that Kennan's separation of morality from national security is damaging to U.S. purposes, and refers to Jefferson and Madison for a historical basis for the belief that "political power must always be restrained by morality." Theodore Weber defends Kennan's intention in the separation of morality from the national interest on the basis of accepted international politics and the danger of elevating U.S. concerns to a messianic crusade. Includes other brief essays by Francis Deng, Richard Joseph, Dayle E. Powell, and a discussion. A reprint of Kennan's article "Morality and Foreign Policy" (no. **545**) is an Appendix. (The volume is the result of a 1989 workshop sponsored by the United States Institute of Peace and the Carter Center of Emory University.)

709. Ninkovich, Frank. "Interests and Discourse in Diplomatic History." *Diplomatic History* 13 (spring 1989): 135-161.

Analyzing the understanding of the national interest in the writings of Charles Beard and George F. Kennan, Ninkovich is critical of both scholars for being "overly objectivist," rendering their arguments against U.S. policy-makers narrow and trivial, and failing to consider "reality in all its breadth."

710. Novak, Michael. "George X. Kennan vs. George Y. Kennan." *Washington Star*, 29 Dec. 1977, sec. A, 7.

A brief article commenting on Kennan's address before the Council on Foreign Relations in 1977 (no. **434**). Novak finds a change in Kennan's estimate of the Soviets from the "X" article (no. **2**), and strongly disagrees with his new-found optimism. Kennan's attitude is an example of "our own elite's loss of heart."

711. Oakes, Guy. "The Cold War Ethic." *International Journal of Politics, Culture, and Society* 61 (1992): 397-404.

Oakes situates Kennan at the heart of a seminal group of policy intellectuals--including John Foster Dulles, Paul Nitze and others--whose focus on Americans' supposed lack of will and moral fibre led them to participate in an "enterprise in moral propaganda and control undertaken by the American state..." early in the Cold War. Oakes highlights Kennan's disgust with urban America and his conviction that a vigorous foreign policy depended upon reasserting traditional core values. Such sentiments lent themselves to a propaganda campaign begun in the Truman Administration, exaggerating Soviet strategic aims and conversely equating U.S. objectives with world salvation.

712. Oliver, Covey T. "Reflections on Two Recent Developments Affecting the Function of Law in the International Community." *Texas Law Review* 30 (Oct. 1952): 815-842.

Written from the perspective of a scholar of international law, Oliver rejects

Kennan's attack on legalism and moralism in the conduct of American foreign policy. He challenges Kennan's specific historical examples and his overall interpretation of legalism made in *American Diplomacy, 1900-1950* (no. **22**). Law is more flexible than Kennan has portrayed it, and it is a useful and necessary force in the conduct of international relations.

713. OTuathail, Gearoid, and John Agnew. "Geopolitics and Discourse: Practical Geopolitical Reasoning in American Foreign Policy." *Political Geography* 11 (Mar. 2, 1992): 190-204.

The authors see Kennan as contributing to a collective "discourse" that reduces foreign affairs to simple, powerful and appealing paradigms. Such is the utility of these to decision-makers, and their persuasiveness to the publics of modern democracies, that they outweigh more complex, partial and conditional judgements based on complex and shifting national interests and the shifting alignments of adversaries and allies.

714. Paterson, Thomas G., ed. *Containment and the Cold War: American Foreign Policy Since 1945*. Reading, Mass.: Addison-Wesley, 1973. 250p.

A collection of articles and excerpts illustrating the background and controversy over the containment policy from 1947 through the 1960s. Authors include, besides Kennan, Walter Lippmann, Dean Acheson, John F. Dulles, William A. Williams, Lloyd C. Gardner, Eduard M. Mark, and J. William Fulbright.

715. ______. "From Architect of Containment to Critic: George F. Kennan and the Soviet Threat." In *Meeting the Communist Threat: From Truman to Reagan*, edited by Thomas G. Paterson, 114-146. New York: Oxford Univ. Press, 1988.

A portrait of Kennan as diplomat, shaper, and critic of U.S. foreign policy toward the Soviets.

716. ______. "The Search for Meaning: George F. Kennan and American Foreign Policy." In *Makers of American Diplomacy*. Vol. 2, *From Theodore Roosevelt to Henry Kissinger*, edited by Frank J. Merli and Theodore A. Wilson, 249-284. New York: Scribner, 1974.

A succinct and thorough biographical essay on Kennan as statesman and scholar.

717. Pfaff, William. "Events Finally Prove Kennan Right." *Manchester Guardian Weekly*, 15 Sept. 1991, 8.

In this short commentary, Pfaff recalls Kennan's prediction, now borne out, that the Soviet state would eventually collapse, and says that the U.S. should also take note of Kennan's advice (in a 1951 article, no. **25**) that when Russia does turn to change, as it has with Boris Yeltsin, the U.S. should not intervene. Pfaff contrasts Kennan's view with that of Henry Kissinger, who took a more activist stance, more in the mainstream of American politics.

718. Pipes, Richard. "Mr. X Revises: A Reply to George Kennan." *Encounter*, Apr. 1978, 18-21.

Responds to a previous article by Kennan, ("Mr. X. Reconsiders" no. **449**). Pipes disagrees that there has been institutional change in the Soviet Union; Kennan and like-minded people fail to see that there is cause for concern in the massive Soviet military build-up taking place. (Reprinted in nos. **634,638**.)

719. Polley, Michael. *A Biography of George F. Kennan: The Education of a Realist.* Lewiston, N.Y.: Edwin Mellen Press, 1990. 178p. (Studies in Twentieth Century American History, v. 4.)

Identifies Kennan as a realist with conservative values, and looks at the impact of his thought. Polley sees continuity in Kennan's positions rather than change. (See also the author's dissertation, no. **778**.)

720. Poole, Peter A. "George Kennan: Author and Critic of the Containment Policy." In *Profiles in American Foreign Policy: Stimson, Kennan, Acheson, Dulles, Rusk, Kissinger and Vance*, by Peter A. Poole, 25-43. Washington, D.C.: University Press of America, 1961.

A brief review of Kennan's early career, beginning in 1944; the genesis of the "Long Telegram" (no. **350**), Kennan's mission to Japan in 1948, and an outline of Kennan's subsequent disagreements with U.S. policies from the 1950s to the 1980s.

721. Powers, Richard J. "Who Fathered Containment?" *International Studies Quarterly* 15 (1971): 526-542.

A review article of the memoirs of Kennan and Arthur Krock, in which Powers compares Kennan's "Long Telegram" (no. **350**) to a memorandum by Clark Clifford, and sees in the Clifford views a closer approximation to the militarist stance subsequently taken by the U.S. in its containment policy.

722. Rosenthal, Joel H. "George F. Kennan, the Atom and the West: Wise Man as Cultural Critic." In *Contemporary Politics: Rhetoric and Discourse*, edited by Kenneth W. Thompson, 237-257. Lanham, Md.: University Press of America, 1988.

An assessment of Kennan as critic of technology and 20th-century culture. Kennan sees no solutions in technology for the world's problems, and he recognizes that the atom bomb brings completely different calculations to international politics.

723. ______. *Righteous Realists: Political Realism, Responsible Power and American Culture in the Nuclear Age*. Baton Rouge: Louisiana Univ. Press, 1991. xxii, 191p.

Looks at five postwar realists--Kennan, Morgenthau, Niebuhr, Lippmann, and Acheson--and argues that their brand of "realism" never advocated simple "power politics" but was an attempt to reconcile moral responsibility with power. (See also his dissertation, no. **781**.)

724. Rostow, Eugene V. "Searching for Kennan's Grand Design." *Yale Law Journal* 87 (June 1978): 1527-1548.

A book review of *The Cloud of Danger* (no. **431**). Rostow calls Kennan an "impressionist, a poet," and he is critical of Kennan's anti-interventionism, which he equates with isolationism and distrust of the democratic process; nevertheless he calls Kennan's work "important." (Reprinted in no. **634**.)

725. Row, Robert. "The Kennan Thesis and the Fate of Europe." *The European*, Mar. 1958, 13-22.

Sir Oswald Mosley (founder of the British Union of Fascists) predicted Soviet military disengagement and a move to political and economic warfare in 1950-1952, nevertheless his ideas were given less recognition in the press than the similar ideas Kennan has expressed recently. Row details the similarities and calls for "a new dynamic" in this political and economic warfare, in which Britain would join with a Europe inclusive of Germany.

726. Ruddy, T. Michael. "Realist versus Realist: Bohlen, Kennan and the Inception of the Cold War." *Midwest Quarterly* 17 (Jan. 1976): 122-141.

Explores the differences in viewpoints and careers of these two Sovietologists. During World War II, Bohlen's analysis emphasized Soviet ideology, while Kennan's emphasized spheres-of-interest and strategy. After the war, they both showed the influence of the other's ideas. Ruddy analyzes their differences over such policies as the Truman Doctrine and NATO.

727. Russell, Greg. "Searching for Realism's Grand Design." *Political Science Reviewer* 19 (1990): 197-245.

Using Kennan's major works on American foreign relations and Russian and European history, Russell sees "conceptual defects in Kennan's realism," and finds that he obscures the values behind his concepts in discussions on morality and foreign policy. Kennan errs on the side of moral relativism and fails to provide guidance on a foreign policy that might be "an instrument of justice." (See also the author's dissertation, no. **782**.)

728. Schlesinger, Arthur., Jr. "The Radical." *New York Review of Books*, 11 Feb. 1993, 3-8.

A review of *Around the Cragged Hill* (no. **591**). Schlesinger characterizes Kennan as a radical thinker with conservative values. He cites Kennan's views on the nation-state, his distaste for extreme nationalism, his doubts that the U.S. "mission" is to spread democracy world-wide, and his proposed solution to the lack of leadership with an appointed "council of state." Schlesinger points out some changes in Kennan's thought over the years.

729. Schoenberger, Howard. "U.S. Policy in Postwar Japan." *Science & Society* 46 (1982): 39-59.

An analysis of the shift in emphasis of U.S. policy in postwar Japan from instituting politically liberal reforms to that of economic reconstruction, in which Kennan played an important role. The policy shift was not, in Schoenberger's view, primarily to counteract a Soviet threat but was part of a broad strategic plan to prevent revolutions in Asia. The expanding Japanese economy was needed in "shoring up the comprador regimes of the region."

730. Seabury, Paul. "George Kennan vs. Mr. 'X': The Great Container Springs a Leak." *New Republic*, 16 Dec. 1981, 17-20.

Argues that containment as originally conceived by Kennan was militaristic. Kennan's recent denials, and his characterization of the Soviet Union as defensive, are mistaken.

731. ______. "Reinspecting Containment." In *Beyond Containment: Alternative American Policies toward the Soviet Union*, edited by Aaron Wildavsky, 39-60. San Francisco: ICS Press, Institute for Contemporary Studies, 1983.

In a historical review of containment policy, Seabury says that Kennan's views in 1947 were "correct and necessary . . . but not sufficient." The U.S. needs to go further with containment policy to encourage contradictions within the Soviet state.

732. Sempa, Francis P. "Geopolitics and American Strategy: A Reassessment." *Strategic*

Review 15 (spring 1987): 27-38.

Relates Kennan's containment thesis to Halford Mackinder's geopolitical theories of the early 1900s. Some critics of containment--James Burnham, Raymond Aron and Nicholas Spykman--have also drawn on Mackinder's geopolitical conceptions. Sempa criticizes arms control advocates for ignoring geopolitical realities and argues that the U.S. needs a global containment strategy.

733. Seton-Watson, Hugh. "George Kennan's Illusions--A Reply." *Encounter*, Nov. 1976, 24-35.

Argues against Kennan's assertions that the West has nothing to offer, and that the U. S. has tried to "Americanize Europe." Contrary to Kennan, the West should aid change in the Soviet Union; the societal problems in the West are not more important than the threat from Soviet imperialism. (Reprinted in nos. **634,638**.)

734. Shimko, Keith L. "Realism, Neorealism, and American Liberalism." *Review of Politics* 54 (spring 1992): 281-301.

Discusses differences in concept between realists and neorealists in international affairs. Shimko argues that neorealists incorporate the American liberal tradition in their thinking, which views international relations as "anarchic," stressing fear of domination. Classical realists, including Kennan, focus on man's propensity for aggrandizement of power and the desire to dominate.

735. Sigal, Leon V. "Kennan's Cuts." *Foreign Policy* 44 (fall 1981): 76-80.

Argues that Kennan's proposal for deep cuts in nuclear arms would be destabilizing, and suggests instead modest reductions and a test ban treaty.

736. Simpson, Dwight J. "New Trends in Foreign Policy: A Criticism of the 'Kennan Thesis.'" *World Affairs Quarterly* 27 (Jan. 1957): 327-343.

Faults Kennan for emphasizing method over goals. Kennan's criticisms of legalism and moralism show little understanding of the use of contracts and power in international politics. His desire to remove foreign policy from popular influence is unrealistic. Containment is a "negative doctrine" that abdicates control over foreign policy, accepts the status quo, and gives little hope to those aspiring to overthrow Communist domination.

737. Siracusa, Joseph M. "Will the Real Author of Containment Please Stand Up: The Strange Case of George Kennan and Frank Roberts." *Society for Historians of Foreign Relations Newsletter* 22 (Sept. 1991): 1-27.

Details the similarities between Kennan's "Long Telegram" (no. **350**) and a dispatch from Kennan's British counterpart in Moscow, Frank Roberts. Siracusa speculates on the influence Roberts may have had on Kennan's analysis of the Soviets.

738. Smith, Michael Joseph. "George Kennan: Diplomacy and Moderation." In *Realist Thought From Weber to Kissinger*, by Michael Joseph Smith, 165-191. Baton Rouge: Louisiana State Univ. Press, 1986.

Outlines themes in Kennan's thought: his realist criticism of U.S. foreign policy, his views on the Soviet Union, and the need for prudent diplomacy and nuclear disarmament. Smith faults containment because it failed to bring about a "mellowing" of the Soviet Union. (See also his dissertation, no. **784**.)

739. Steel, Ronald. "Guest of the Age." *New York Review of Books*, 17 Aug. 1989, 3-5.
A review of Kennan's *Sketches from a Life* (no. **564**) and the biographies by Mayers (no. **699**) and Stephanson (no. **742**). Steel discusses Kennan's detachment, conservatism and romanticism--characteristics that make him a critic of "coruscating clarity" and an ineffective bureaucrat.

740. ______. "Man Without a Country." In *Imperialists and Other Heroes: A Chronicle of the American Empire*, by Ronald Steel, 38-57. New York: Random House, 1971.
A portrait of Kennan drawn from his *Memoirs, 1925-1950* (no. **306**), his influence in and out of the State Department, his views of the Soviet Union and Germany, and his elitism and feelings of personal isolation.

741. ______. "The Statesman of Survival." *Esquire*, Jan. 1985, 68-75.
Gives a synopsis of Kennan's career and foreign policy issues he has written about --the Soviet Union, Eastern Europe, and Germany--as well as his alienation from contemporary society and his elitism. Steele interviewed Kennan on the subject of his support for the antinuclear movement. He praises him for taking a long view as a historian and critic.

742. Stephanson, Anders. *Kennan and the Art of Foreign Policy*. Cambridge, Mass.: Harvard Univ. Press, 1989. x, 380p.
Emphasizing "text over context," Stephanson studies three aspects of Kennan's thought: his views of the Soviet Union, 1930-1950, his concept of the national interest, and his view of American culture, to better understand U.S. foreign policy in the Cold War. The book gives a detailed analysis of Kennan's thought and influence. Stephanson finds that Kennan's views on the Soviets contributed to the limitations of "perceived policy options" considered by the U.S. (See also his dissertation, no. **785**.)

743. ______. "Kennan's Lament: American Mass Culture Uncontained." *New Perspectives Quarterly* 6 (fall 1989): 54-57.
Shows, with a series of quotations from Kennan, his unhappiness with modern-day America, the vicarious experiences of mass-media marketing, undifferentiated sense of place from mass-consumer chains, and the harmful ecological effects of unlimited technological development and self-interest. Stephanson contrasts Kennan's sensibility to that of another cultural critic, Herbert Marcuse, who identified American mass-culture as a liberation from tradition and established power-structures. Kennan's criticisms were those of an "'organicist' or Burkean conservative, for whom the operative notion is ritual and tradition."

744. Stillman Edmund. "Containment Has Won, But." *New York Times Magazine*, 28 May 1967, 23+.
Argues that containment meant by Kennan in the "X" article (no. **2**) was defensive but not passive, and that containment policy in the Truman Doctrine was not global. It was the Korean War which produced a "universalized . . . rigid doctrine" and "sham alliances." Soviet rhetoric also contributed to solidifying the Cold War, contrary to what Kennan had intended.

745. Taft, John. "Grey Eminences, X. A Diplomat for the Eighties." *New Republic*, 17 Mar. 1979, 19-21.
A brief profile of Kennan commenting on his scholarly and political activities after

leaving the State Dept., including the Reith Lectures, Kennan's views on colonialism, detente, and Vietnam. In Taft's view, Kennan's affinity for the "establishment of a century ago--1880," contributes to his lack of understanding of present-day politics and his strange mixture of liberalism and conservatism.

746. Thompson, Kenneth W. "George F. Kennan: The War on Legalism and Moralism." In *Masters of International Thought: Major Twentieth Century Theorists and the World Crisis*, 143-158. Baton Rouge: Louisiana State Univ. Press, 1980.

Illustrates Kennan's philosophy with reference to his major works, gives a synopsis of the genesis of the "X" article (no. **2**), and discusses some of his disagreements with Acheson and Dulles. Thompson calls Kennan's recommendations on European policy "prophetic," given recent German moves toward *Ostpolitik* and U.S. endorsement of the Helsinki accords. Kennan, despite his strictures against "moralism" in foreign policy, is a moral thinker.

747. ______. "The Kennan-Acheson Debate." *Commonweal*, 4 Apr. 1958, 6-9.

Reviewing Kennan's *Russia, the Atom and the West* (no. **136**) and Dean Acheson's *Power and Diplomacy*, Thompson finds the two books clearly show the differences of opinion on specific policies such as NATO, Central Europe, and the Soviet Union. He characterizes these differences as a clash between a military and diplomatic view of the Cold War, "between concepts that have worked tolerably well for at least a decade and views that foreshadow new events."

748. Trask, Roger R. "George F. Kennan's Report on Latin America (1950)." *Diplomatic History* 2 (summer 1978): 307-311.

Discusses a memorandum on policy in Latin America written by Kennan in 1950 (published in 1976 in *Foreign Relations of the United States*, no. **427**). Trask disagrees with Kennan's analysis, and with the conclusion that the area is not a "vital interest."

749. Treadgold, Donald W. "The Future of Communism: George Kennan's Neo-Isolationism." *New Leader*, 3 Sept. 1956, 9-11.

Replying to Kennan's article in a previous issue, "The Future of Soviet Communism" (no. **101**), Treadgold faults Kennan for the absence of moral support for resistance movements in the U.S.S.R and the satellite countries, and for his analysis of the domestic political scene in these countries.

750. Ulam, Adam B. "Cold War According to Kennan." *Commentary*, Jan. 1973, 66-69.

Reviewing Kennan's *Memoirs* (no. **306**), Ulam challenges Kennan's interpretation of Soviet intentions in the early Cold War years, and of the possibilities for negotiation after Stalin's death.

751. Ullman, R. H. "The Realities of George F. Kennan." *Foreign Policy* 28 (fall 1977): 39-155.

An essay review of *The Cloud of Danger* (no. **431**), in which Ullman summarizes Kennan's views on foreign policy since 1950, agreeing that there is a need for realism over ideology and rhetoric but faulting Kennan for avoiding hard problems in his assessment of U.S. policies toward the Third World.

752. Walsh, Peter Gerard. "Advice from a Prophet." *International Perspectives* (Canada) (May-June 1983): 11-14.

Reviewing *The Nuclear Delusion* (no. **513**), Walsh briefly discusses Kennan's views. He takes issue with Kennan's conclusions about Soviet capabilities, but calls his recognition of the danger of nuclear weapons and the arms race "sobering."

753. Weise, Eric. "Mr. 'X,' Russia, and Vietnam." *Modern Age* 19 (fall 1975): 397-406.
The policy of containment put forth in the "X" article (no. **2**), has been successful, in spite of Kennan's disavowal of it, and the outcome of the war in Vietnam finalizes this success, with both the Soviets and the Chinese backing off from wars of liberation.

754. Whelan, Joseph. G. "George Kennan and His Influence on American Foreign Policy." *Virginia Quarterly Review* 35 (spring 1959): 196-220.
Whelan sees a discontinuity in Kennan's policy recommendations from containment to disengagement, and he faults Kennan the realist for being unrealistic in his proposals for disengagement.

755. Williams, William Appleman. "A Second Look at Mr. X." In *History as a Way of Learning: Articles, Excerpts and Essays*, by William Appleman Williams, 105-114. New York: New Viewpoints, 1973.
Written in 1952 when Kennan was appointed Ambassador to Moscow (and originally published in *Monthly Review*), Williams examines Kennan's understanding of the Soviet Union and of U.S. diplomacy, and is critical of his views: particularly Kennan's lack of attention to the "fundamental challenge" to the West that the Bolshevik Revolution presented, and his omission of the economic aspects of foreign policy. Kennan has never explicitly abandoned containment, a basically militaristic policy.

756. Wright, C. Ben. "Mr. X and Containment." *Slavic Review* 35 (Jan. 1976): 1-31.
Argues that the "X" article (no. **2**), and other statements of Kennan at the time, supported militarism and globalism in U.S. foreign policy, contrary to Kennan's later assertions that these aspects were misinterpretations of his conception of containment.

757. "'X' Plus 25." *Foreign Policy* 7 (summer 1972): 3-53.
An interview (see no. **383**), reprint of the "X" article (no. **2**), and critiques by Charles Gati, "What Containment Meant" and Chalmers M. Roberts, "How Containment Worked." (See also, Gati, *Caging the Bear* no. **650**).

758. "The X, Y, Z Affair." *The Nation*, 5 Feb. 1990, 149.
An editorial commenting on an article in the Winter 1990 issue of *Daedalus* by "Z," which argues that Gorbachev's reforms will not succeed in desired changes in the Soviet Union, and that U.S. aid should be cut off. This editorial argues that the "Z" article has misappropriated Kennan's containment concept.

759. Yergin, Daniel. *Shattered Peace: The Origins of the Cold War and the National Security State*. Boston: Houghton, Mifflin, 1977. x, 526p.
Although Kennan is not a central figure in this work as a whole, he does play an important role as an adherent of the "Riga Axioms," post-World War II policy-makers who, in Yergin's categorization, advocated a hardline policy toward the Soviet Union, in contrast to those who favored the "Yalta Axioms," signifying an

approach emphasizing diplomacy and coexistence. However, Yergin describes Kennan by 1950, as "a critic, rather than a promulgator, of the Riga axioms."

760. Zimmerman, William. "Rethinking Soviet Foreign Policy: Changing American Perspectives." *International Journal* (Canada) 35 (winter 1979/1980): 548-562.
Briefly mentions Kennan's "X" article (no. 2) in an analysis differentiating U.S. policies toward the Soviet Union from the point of view of the perceived effects of U.S. actions.

DISSERTATIONS

761. Ball-Kilburne, Gary Lee. *Conceptualizing the Enemy: An Exploration Into the Moral Discourse Over Nuclear Weapons.* Ph.D. diss., Vanderbilt Univ., 1988. 275p.
(Not seen.)

762. Brinkley, Douglas. *Dean Acheson: Elder Statesman of the Cold War, 1953-1971.* Ph.D. diss., Georgetown Univ., 1989. 735p.
(Not seen.)

763. Callan, Theresa Ellen-Marie. *A Study in American Realism.* Ph.D. diss., Queen's University of Belfast (Northern Ireland), 1994.
(Not seen.)

764. Coffey, John William. *Realist Social Thought in America: Reinhold Niebuhr and George F. Kennan.* Ph.D. diss., Stanford University, 1971. 512p.
(Not seen.)

765. Denman, Dorothy Irene. *The Riddle of Containment: As Reflected in the Advice and Dissent of George F. Kennan.* Ph.D. diss., University of Miami, 1975. 316p.
(Not seen.)

766. Edwards, Elizabeth Leila. *Truman, Containment and the Cold War.* Ph.D. diss, Univ. of Virginia, 1994. 376p.
(Not seen.)

767. Epp, Roger Ivan. *Power Politics and the "Civitas Terrena": The Augustinian Sources of Anglo-American Thought in International Relations.* Ph.D. diss., Queens Univ. at Kingston (Canada), 1990. 420p.
(Not seen.)

768. Finkelstein, David Michael. *From Abandonment to Salvation: The Evolution of United States Policy Toward Taiwan, 1949-1950.* Ph.D. diss., Princeton University, 1990. 588p.

(Not seen.)

769. Green, James Frederick. *The Political Thought of George F. Kennan: A Study of the Development and Interrelations of American and Soviet Foreign Policies.* Ph.D. diss., American University, 1972. 397p.

Green analyzes theoretical contradictions in Kennan's thought in this study of his views on U.S. and Soviet foreign policies. Categorizing Kennan as an "activist-organicist," Green sees a change in his thinking after 1948-1949, when he began to emphasize the "organicist" or societal factors over the "activist" or individual actions. This shift led Kennan to overemphasize political containment.

770. Harrington, Virginia Marie. *The Quest for Consensus: U.S.-Soviet Relations, 1949-1952.* Ph.D. diss., Cornell Univ., 1987. 363p.

(Not seen.)

771. Heer, Paul James. *George F. Kennan and U.S. Foreign Policy in East Asia.* Ph.D. diss., George Washington Univ., 1995. 375p.

(Not seen.)

772. Hindle, Robert Earl. *George Kennan and the Beginnings of Containment.* Ph.D. diss., Claremont Graduate School, 1970. 217p.

Examines the policy of containment as expressed by Kennan in the "X" article (no. **2**) and the "Long Telegram" (no. **350**), differences between Kennan and the Truman administration's policies, and the range of contemporary criticisms of containment in the 1950s. Kennan's expressions were too ambiguous to succeed on his terms; but the Truman version also failed in understanding Soviet purposes.

773. Hixson, Walter Lawrence. *From Containment to Neo-Isolation: The Diplomacy of George F. Kennan, 1944-1957.* Ph.D. diss., University of Colorado at Boulder, 1986. 420p.

(Not seen. Cf. his book on Kennan, no. **664**.)

774. Hood, Donald Eugene. *"Lessons" of the Vietnam War: Henry Kissinger, George F. Kennan, Richard Falk and the Debate over Containment, 1965-1980.* Ph.D. diss., University of Washington, 1982. 284p.

The chapter on Kennan looks at his views on U.S. foreign policy, the Soviet Union and the Cold War, and his criticisms of the Vietnam War. Hood finds Kennan's criticisms trenchant, and his opposition to the Vietnam War courageous, but feels he underestimated the importance of Soviet interventions and military strength.

775. Kallina, Edmund Frank, Jr. *A Conservative Criticism of American Foreign Policy: The Publications and Careers of Louis J. Halle, George F. Kennan, and Charles Burton Marshall, 1950-1968.* Ph.D. diss., Northwestern University, 1970. 331p.

(Not seen.)

776. McIntyre, A. Dan. *Political Discourse and the U.S. National Interest: Three Great Transformations (United States, Federalist Papers, Foreign Policy).* Ph.D. diss., Princeton University, 1991. 172p.

(Not seen.)

777. Miscamble, Wilson Douglas. *George F. Kennan, the Policy Planning Staff, and American Foreign Policy, 1947-1950*. Ph.D. diss., University of Notre Dame, 1980. 265p.

A detailed study of the positions of the State Department's Policy Planning Staff, when Kennan was its Director, and competing views on key foreign policy issues after World War II--the Marshall Plan, formation of NATO, Germany, and development and control of nuclear weapons. Miscamble assesses the role of the PPS in policy-making. (See also his book, no. **706**.)

778. Polley, Michael John. *George F. Kennan: The Life and Times of a Diplomat, 1925-1975*. Ph.D. diss., Washington State University, 1984. 777p.

(Not seen. Cf. his book on Kennan, no. **719**.)

779. Powers, Richard James. *Kennan Against Himself? From Containment to Disengagement, a Decade of U.S. Foreign Policy-Making as Focused on the Ideas and Concepts of George F. Kennan, 1947-1957*. Ph.D. diss., Claremont Graduate School, 1967. 250p.

(Not seen.)

780. Reed., Laura W. *The Roads Not Taken: The United States Security Debate Over Germany, 1944-1949*. Ph.D. diss., Massachusetts Institute of Technology, 1995.

(Not seen.)

781. Rosenthal, Joel Howard. *Righteous Realists: Perceptions of American Power and Responsibility in the Nuclear Age*. Ph.D. diss., Yale University, 1988. 349p.

(Not seen. Cf. his book, no. **723**.)

782. Russell, Gregory T. *Raison D'Etat and the American Philosophy of Realism in World Affairs*. Ph.D. diss., Louisiana State University and Agricultural and Mechanical College, 1987. 548p. (2 v.)

In the chapter on Kennan, Russell discusses Kennan's position on morality in international relations, and finds it hard to define and contradictory; he categorizes Kennan as a "moral relativist." (Cf. article no. **727**.)

783. Salmon, Jeffrey Talley. *The Statesmanship of Dean Acheson*. Ph.D. diss., Catholic Univ. of America, 1985. 294p.

(Not seen.)

784. Smith, Michael Joseph. *Realism as an Approach to International Relations: A Critical Analysis*. Ph.D. diss., Harvard University, 1982. 417p.

(Not seen.)

785. Stephanson, Anders Gunnar Ernst. *Kennan: Art and Foreign Policy*. Ph.D. diss., Columbia University, 1987. 530p.

(Not seen. Cf. his book on Kennan, no. **742**.)

786. Underhill-Cady, Joseph B. *Doing Battle With Death: United States Foreign Policy Elite and the Discourse on War, 1898-1968*. Ph.D. diss., Univ. of Michigan, 1995. 450p.

(Not seen.)

787. Wright, C. Ben. *George F. Kennan, Scholar-Diplomat: 1926-1946.* Ph.D. diss., University of Wisconsin-Madison, 1972. 512p.

An in-depth study of Kennan's early career and an analysis of his thought and influence through 1946. Wright admires Kennan's good sense and intellect and his subtle analysis of the Soviet Union, but finds him emotional and not explicit enough in his policy recommendations. Wright attempts an understanding of Kennan's complexities. (See also no. **607**.)

NAME/TITLE INDEX

SUBJECT INDEX

About the Compiler

LAUREL F. FRANKLIN is associate professor and head of the Catalog Division in the Library Department at the City College of CUNY.

CPSIA information can be obtained at www.ICGtesting.com
Printed in the USA
BVOW06*2013191016

465513BV00008B/133/P

9 780313 283062